Fly-Tying Illustrated–

wet and dry patterns

Freddie Rice

*Member of the Association of Professional
Game Angling Instructors – Fly Dressing*

*National Angling Council Instructor,
Grade I, including Fly Dressing Trout and Salmon*

B. T. Batsford Ltd, London

First published 1981
© Freddie Rice 1981, 1985
First published in paperback 1985
Reprinted 1986

ISBN 0 7134 2364 1

Illustrations and photographs by the Author

Filmset in Times Roman 10 on 12 pt. by
Elliott Bros & Yeoman Ltd,
Speke, Liverpool L24 9JL
Printed and bound in Great Britain by
Anchor Brendon Ltd, Tiptree, Essex
for the publishers B. T. Batsford Ltd,
4 Fitzhardinge Street, London WIH 0AH

Contents

Acknowledgments   5

'On Flies' by John Gay   6

1 The Delusive Art   7

2 Tools and Materials   32
    Tools   34
    Miscellaneous Aids   36
    Hooks   37
    Threads, Tinsels, Wires, Wax and Varnish   42
    Materials   46
    Capes (or Rooster Necks)   52
    Picric Acid   57

3 Ways and Means   59

4 Patterns   69
    Wet Flies   70
    Dry Flies   120

'On Colour' by James Ogden   170

Bibliography *and Other Books of Interest*   171

Index   173

Acknowledgments

My thanks are due to many friends and others, more than I can mention here, who have, in their own way, contributed to these pages, and it gives me great pleasure to acknowledge my debt to them, particularly to:

Sue Hodgson, beginning only her second year of fly-tying, who dressed many of the patterns illustrated;

Dick Walker, whose informative letters to Maurice Ingham in *Drop me a Line* initiated my interest in fly-tying;

Taff Price, photographic genius, for technical guidance and for the loan of his headache;

John Veniard Limited and Mustad and Son for permission to quote from their catalogues;

My students who have, over many years, helped me to understand the problems of the beginner and who have been the source of many new ideas.

My son, Graham, for very helpful advice and encouragement;

My wife, for profound patience in typing and arranging the manuscript, without whose help it would never have been completed.

Thank you all.

Freddie Rice
Long Ditton
May, 1980

ON FLIES

But when the sun displays his glorious beams,
And shallow rivers flow with silver streams,
Then the deceit the scaly breed survey,
Bask in the sun, and look into the day.
You now a more delusive art must try,
And tempt their hunger with the curious fly.
  To frame the little animal, provide
All the gay hues that wait on female pride,
Let Nature guide thee; sometimes golden wire
The shining bellies of the fly require;
The peacock plumes thy tackle must not fail,
Nor the dear purchase of the sable's tail.
Each gaudy bird some slender tribute brings,
And lends the growing insect proper wings:
Silks of all colours must their aid impart,
And every fur promote the fisher's art.
So the gay lady, with expensive care,
Borrows the pride of land, of sea, and air;
Furs, pearls, and plumes, the glittering thing displays,
Dazzles our eyes, and easy hearts betrays.
  Mark well the various seasons of the year,
How the succeeding insect race appear;
In this revolving moon one colour reigns,
Which in the next the fickle trout disdains.
Oft have I seen a skilful angler try
The various colours of the treacherous fly;
When he with fruitless pain hath skimm'd the brook,
And the coy fish rejects the skipping hook,
He shakes the boughs that on the margin grow,
Which o'er the stream a waving forest throw;
When, if an insect fall (his certain guide),
He gently takes him from the whirling tide;
Examines well his form, with curious eyes,
His gaudy vest, his wings, his horns and size.
Then round his hook the chosen fur he winds,
And on the back a speckled feather binds,
So just the colours shine through every part,
That Nature seems to live again in Art.

John Gay (1685–1732)

1

The Delusive Art

The earliest evidence of any attempt to catch fish using an artificial fly seems to be that of Aelian (Claudius Aelianus) (AD 170–235) of Praeneste, Italy. In his *De natura animalium,* a collection of animal stories often pointing a moral, he refers to the use by the Macedonians of a fly having a body made of red wool to which was added 'two feathers which grow under a cock's wattle,' presumably describing a neck hackle from a domestic fowl. Note that it is a cock's hackle, one usually found to be stiff in the fibre eminently suitable for a *floating* fly rather than for a sunk fly where a softer hackle with more web would be more easily worked upon by the current. Whether or not this was a 'dry fly' it is interesting to speculate why, and by what process of experience, red was found to be the most advantageous, a colour still considered beneficial, as witness the tag in Red Tag, the tail in Silver Butcher and the ever popular Red and Soldier Palmers.

Unfortunately, Aelian does not say whether, in the fly he describes, the hackle is tied in at the head only or wound down the length of the shank palmerwise. However, it seems likely that the Red Hackle, whatever its form, is the earliest pattern known to us.

A vast gap seems to exist from Aelian's time to the fifteenth century before further written evidence appears concerning artificial flies, although the American Indians are reputed to have made and used flies made from deer hair, a hollow material with good floating properties. Did this material come into use because a floating form was sought or because the hair happened to be freely available? The flies are said to have been made by cutting a very slim strip of skin which was then attached to some form of elementary hook. If wound on, this process would make the hair flare out from the hook shank very much in the manner of a palmered hackle, which these drawings illustrate (fig. 1).

Printing on movable type worked by John Gutenberg of Mainz in about 1450 was carried to London in 1477 and whilst the spread of the new art of printing was at first mainly confined to religious and classical works, it was not long before other subjects appeared. Although the first edition of the *Boke of St Albans,* ascribed to Dame Juliana Berners, was printed in 1486 it deals mainly with hawking and hunting and a further ten years passed before Wynkyn de Worde, successor to Caxton at Westminster, printed the second edition which included the 'Treatyse of Fysshynge wyth an Angle,' the first known work on angling in the English language. It lists twelve flies which are set out for use month by month and it is clear, I feel, that they are the product of evolution rather than the invention, at the time, of Dame Juliana, then Prioress of Sopwell Nunnery at St Albans. The listing month by month is surely an indication that the flies were attempts, however crude, to provide passable representations of the natural flies which would be on the water during the months of March to August, the relative month being named above each fly described.

1   Comparison of palmered hackle and palmered hair on skin

Whilst not all the dozen are easily identifiable, of those given for March one is a fair description of the March Brown and the other possibly the Olive Dun. For April, the Stonefly and the Great Red Spinner, whilst for May a Mayfly or Yellow May Dun. The fly for June is described as the 'donne cutte,' apparently a sedge. This name has a familiar ring in Charles Cotton's Dun Cut but the latter fly is provided with horns absent in the former. For the same month the Alder Fly is given and either the Dung Fly or, possibly, the Oak Fly; for July the 'waspe flye' and the Grannom or a similar insect. The twelfth, listed for August, is in doubt. Perhaps you can decipher the intention of 'The drake flye, the body of blacke wull & lappyd abowte wyth blacke sylke: wynges of the mayle of the blacke drake wyth a blacke heed.' The materials, wool, silk and feather, are still favoured in fly-tying although nearly five hundred years have passed sinced the 'Treatyse' was published.

A number of our natural flies are also present on the Continent and it could be that some, at least, of the dressings given in the 'Treatyse' are the result of outside influence for, after all, communication with France was increasing. In this connection it is interesting to note that although the work originated in the south-east of England and gives, in the first dressing, a description of the March Brown, this fly is not known to inhabit the streams in this area but it is found on rivers in Normandy. However, the important thing is that this volume is the baseline from which fly-tying has progressed and developed over the centuries and is still developing today.

It is accepted that angling for all fish was fairly widespread practice even in the fifteenth century and after the 'Treatyse' there followed a number of books on angling in general among which, in 1590, came *A Booke of Fishing with Hooke and Line* by Leonard Mascall with fresh views on making flies with cork bodies and the first to refer to the use of double hooks. Ten years later was published *Certaine Experiments concerning Fish and Fruite: Practised by John Taverner, Gentleman, by him published for the benefit of others.* Taverner was Surveyor of the King's Woods south of the Trent, son of Roger Taverner, Verderer of the Royal Forest of Epping and a very observant and practical man who knew, by observation, that the beliefs prevalent at the time, namely that flies were bred from mud, or corruption, or may-dew or other fanciful notions, were bunkum. Some fanciful notions still exist. My son recently talked to a country workman who was convinced it was in the natural order of things that minnows came down with the rain. This, he seriously contended, accounted for those he found in an old sink in his garden. Taverner looked, noted and learned from nature, ignoring superstition and fantasy. He observed the ephemera nymph transposing into imago and whilst he does not actually refer to the splitting open of the shuck, it seems clear from what he writes that this is what he saw. Major J. W. Hills, in his now classic work, *A History of Fly-fishing for Trout* (1921) quotes Taverner as saying:

> I have seene a young flie swimme in the water too and fro, and in the end come to the upper crust of the water, and assay to flie up: howbeit not being perfitly ripe or fledge, hath twice or thrice fallen downe againe into the water: howbeit in the end receiving perfection by the heate of the sunne, and the pleasant fat water, hath in the ende within halfe houre taken her flight, and flied quite awaie into the ayre. And of such young flies before they are able to flie awaie, do fish feede exceedingly.

It is a pity that a naturalist of such perception did not write more on the subject.

Not until 1651 did another book appear which sets out instructions for dressing trout flies. *The Art of Angling* is by Thomas Barker, a modest, down-to-earth man making no claims to literacy and offering apologies 'for not writing Scholler like.' Yet he is obviously an experienced angler

and fly-dresser, anxious to share his knowledge which, he says, he has
'been gathering these fifty years . . . having spent many pounds in the
gaining thereof.' There is no doubt that he knew his business, as the following extract shows.

> Wee will begin to make the Palmer Flie: You must arm your Line on
> the inside of the hook; take your Scisers and cut so much of the brown
> of the Mallards feather, as in your own reason shall make the wings,
> then lay the outmost part of the feather next the hook, and the poynt of
> the feather towards the shank of the hook, then whip it three or four
> times about the hook with the same silk you armed the hook; then
> make your silk fast; then you must take the hackle of the neck of a Cock
> or Capon, or a Plovers top, which is the best; take off the one side of the
> feather; then you must take the hackle silk, or cruell, gold, or silver,
> thred; make all these fast at the bent of the hook, then you must begin
> with cruell, and silver, or gold, and work it up to the wings, every bout
> shifting your fingers and making a stop, then the gold will fall right,
> then make fast; then work up the hackle to the same place, then make
> the hackle fast; then your must take the hook betwixt your finger and
> thumb, in the left hand, with a neeld or pin, part the wings in two; then
> with the arming silk, as you have fastened all hitherto, whip about as it
> falleth crosse betwixt the wings, then with your thumb you must turn
> the poynt of the feather towards the bent of the hook; then work three
> or four times about the shank; so fasten; then view the proportion.

Whereas the 'Treatyse' hardly touches on the tying processes, generally
setting out little more than the materials recommended for use, Barker
gives the first known instruction on how actually to tie the fly including
reference to the figure-of-eight binding to keep the wings apart,
described as 'whip it about as it falleth crosse betwixt the wings,' and ending with the artistic touch – 'then view the proportion.'

It is an exceedingly interesting and informative book, written with confidence and based an acute observation of natural flies which enable him
to advise on the times of emergence of the naturals and to include helpful
hints such as 'Note, the lightest of your Flies for cloudie and darknesse
and the darkest of your Flies for lightnesse,' and also advises 'observing
the times and seasons.' Walton thought enough of this book to borrow
from it for his second and subsequent editions of the Compleat Angler.

Barker's book was reprinted and enlarged in 1657 under the agreeable
title of Barker's Delight when he must have been in the twilight of his
years, for in the 'Epistle to the Reader' in the first publication (1651) he
writes, 'for I am grown old.' I would like to think that he received due
acclaim from his contemporaries for the practical information his book
contains.

Meantime, in 1653, Izaak Walton published the first edition of his *Compleat Angler* from which so many editions have followed. Walton was an all-round angler who had experience not only of coarse fish but also of trout and salmon, pollution not having bespoiled the rivers and streams as has since occurred. This book is mainly concerned with the taking of coarse fish but the later editon of *Compleat Angler* published in 1676 when Walton had reached the ripe old age of 83, incorporates as the second part the contribution by Charles Cotton, a north countryman. Cotton's part of the work includes precise details of how to go about dressing a winged fly, thus:

In making a fly, then, which is not a hackle or palmer fly (for of those, and their several kinds, we shall have occasion to speak every month in the year), you are, first, to hold your hook fast betwixt the forefinger and thumb of your left hand, with the back of the shank upwards, and the point towards your fingers' ends; then take a strong small silk of the colour of the fly you intend to make, wax it well with wax of the same colour too, to which end you are always, by the way, to have wax of all colours about you, and draw it betwixt your finger and thumb to the head of the shank; and then whip it twice or thrice about the bare hook, which your must know, is done, both to prevent slipping, and also that the shank of the hook may not cut the hairs of your towght, which sometimes it will otherwise do. Which being done, take your line, and draw it likewise betwixt your finger and thumb, holding the hook so fast as only to suffer it to pass by, until you have the knot of your towght almost to the middle of the shank of your hook, on the inside of it; then whip your silk twice or thrice about both hook and line as hard as the strength of the silk will permit. Which being done, strip the feather for the wings proportionable to the bigness of your fly, placing that side downwards which grew uppermost before upon the back of the hook, leaving so much only as to serve for the length of the wing of the point of the plume lying reversed from the end of the shank upwards: then whip your silk twice or thrice about the root-end of the feather, hook, and towght; which being done, clip off the root-end of the feather close by the arming, and then whip the silk fast and firm about the hook and towght, until you come to the bend of the hook, but not further, as you do at London, and so make a very unhandsome, and, in plain English, a very unnatural and shapeless fly. Which being done, cut away the end of your towght and fasten it. And then take your dubbing which is to make the body of your fly, as much as you think convenient, and holding it lightly, with your hook, betwixt the finger and thumb of your left hand, take your silk with the right, and twisting it betwixt the finger and thumb of that hand, the dubbing will spin itself about the silk, which

when it has done, whip it about the armed hook backward, till you
come to the setting-on of the wings. And then take the feather for the
wings, and divide it equally into two parts; and turn them back towards
the bend of the hook, the one on the one side, and the other on the
other of the shank; holding them fast in that posture betwixt the forefinger and thumb of your left hand: which done, warp them so down as
to stand and slope towards the bend of the hook; and having warped up
to the end of the shank, hold the fly fast betwixt the finger and thumb of
your right hand; and where the warping ends pinch or nip it with your
thumb nail against your finger, and strip away the remainder of your
dubbing from the silk; and then with the bare silk whip it once or twice
about; make the wings to stand in due order; fasten, and cut it off. After
which, with the point of a needle, raise up the dubbing gently from the
warp; twitch off the superfluous hairs of your dubbing; leave the wings
of an equal length, your fly will never else swim true; and the work is
done.

Notice that the fingers are used as a vice and for holding materials we
would manipulate with hackle pliers.

Cotton lists 65 flies, by no means all of which can be considered original, but certainly many would prove to be taking flies if used today and,
what is more, would be recognised by name – the Green Drake, Stone
Fly, Black Gnat and the Blue Dun, for instance. He covers many aspects
of fly-tying and the relevant materials and a number of the descriptions
seem to be based, not only on examination of the natural fly, but also of its
habits. For instance, the third fly described for February –

3.   Also a LESSER HACKLE, with a black body, also silver twist
over that, and a red feather over all, will fill your pannier, if the month
be open, and not bound up in ice and snow, with very good fish; but in
case of a frost and snow, you are to angle only with the smallest gnats,
browns, and duns you can make; and with those are only to expect
Graylings no bigger than sprats.

For February he specifies eight flies, seven each for March and April, 16
for May, 12 for June, seven for July, four for August and two for September. For October he opines that flies for March are taken, whilst for
November those for February. For December he concludes, 'at its best, it
is hardly worth a man's labour.'

Cotton's riverside observations made him realise that the fish view the
fly against the light, hence he counsels that the colours of silks and dubbing need particular care in the selection and that 'a bright sunshine day'
is best for fly-tying when the true colour of the dubbing may be judged by
its appearance against strong light. Such observations indicate a percep-

tive and thinking man and it is not surprising that his work has endured despite the publication by James Chetham of Smedley, in 1681, of *The Angler's Vade Mecum* which, without any reference to Cotton, incorporated the latter's fly lists and fly-dressing instructions. However, Chetham includes a second list of patterns which seems original, showing a predominance of dubbed bodies but also introducing the first reference to the use of starling primary or secondary wing quills for the wings of artificial flies. For his September fly, the Little Blue Dun, he incorporates this advice: 'Note, that the Feather got from the Quills, or Pens of Shepstares Wings, Throstle Wings, Fieldfare Wings are generally better (the 2 first especially) to use for Dub-fly Wings, than those got from a wild Mallard, or Drake,' the Shepstare being the starling, whereas previously both Barker and Cotton favoured mallard.

Then, again, he is the first to indicate, in his fly for June, the Sandy Fly, the use of a 'feather from a Herons Neck' for the body of the fly, a material still popular today. With regard to materials, a substantial list necessary to the angler is provided which includes hair from bears, camels, badgers and spaniels, hair from abortive colts and calves, fur from squirrels, black cat's tail, hare's neck, white weasel's tail, mole, yellow rabbit, martern's yellow fur and fur from ferrets. On feathers in his materials list he advises –

Feathers of all sort of Fowls, and of all colours, as Feathers on the Back, and other parts of the wild Mallard, or Drake, and Feathers of a Partridge, and of a Partridge-Tail, and Feathers of a Brown Hen, Throstle-wing, and Feathers got from the Quills and Pens of the wings of Shepstares, Stares or Starling, Fieldfare, and Throstle. The Peacocks Herle, Feathers of a Herons Neck, the top or Cop of a Plover, or Lapwing, which will make the Black Gnat, the Black Feather of an Ostridge or Estridge, and those of various Dyed colours, which Children and others wear in Caps, Feathers from Quills in a Blackbirds Wing and Tail, the Black Down of a Water-coot, and Feathers of all other Colours and Birds, etc.

Yet, practical though all this is, Chetham was credulous enough to believe in concoctions of 'Man's Fat' or 'the powdered Bones or Skull of a dead Man' with which to annoint his bait, reminiscent of the ingredients required for their cauldron by the witches in *Macbeth*. In fairness, however, it must be said that Chetham did advance the knowledge and practice of fly-tying.

From Chetham's time on no doubt other literary offerings on angling were published, but our next milestone is *The Art of Angling* by Richard and Charles Bowlker, father and son. The precise date of publication is uncertain; one authoritative catalogue lists it as 1747. The book, which is more of a manual, provides instruction on fly-dressing and month-by-month advice on the flies to be used. It is written in a direct and simple style making the subject easy to understand and there is a wealth of entomological detail which, no doubt, contributed to the book's success, several editions being published.

It begins with a list of the flies which, one assumes, had been in use up to that date described by the authors as 'flies that are not worth the angler's notice' and continues 'and so to proceed to those that are more useful.' In the 19 listed, to which the first comment relates, we find No. 18 to be 'Harry Long Legs,' our present-day Daddy Long Legs, the Crane Fly. Many are flies described in the 'Treatyse' whilst others are given by Cotton. The Wasp, or 'Waspe,' for instance, appears in both yet 'out with it' say the Bowlkers. They offer, instead of the earlier 19, a fresh list of 29 flies, followed by a description of each, in some cases quite detailed, clearly indicating that the writers had closely observed the naturals they were copying. Take their description of 'The Brown Fly or Dun Drake.'

> Comes down the beginning of March, and continues till the middle of April: His wings are made of the feather of a pheasant's wing, which is full of fine shade, and exactly resembles the wing of the fly: The body is made of the bright part of hare's fur, mixed with a little of the red part of squirrel's fur, ribbed with yellow silk, and a partridge's hackle wrapt twice or thrice under the but of the wing: As he swims down the water, his wings stand upright upon his back, his tail is forked, the colour of his wings: He comes upon the water about eleven o'clock, and continues till two, appearing upon the water in shoals or great quantities; in dark gloomy days, at the approach of the least gleam of sun, it is amazing to see, in a moment's time, the surface of the water almost covered over with ten thousand of these pretty little flying insects, and the fish rising and sporting at them, insomuch that you would think the whole river was alive; a pleasant sight to the angler, and affords him great diversion; in this manner they appear upon the water every successive day, till the end of their duration. The Blue Dun, and the Brown, are both on at the same time, the blues are most plentiful in cold and dark days, and the browns in warm and gloomy days, tho' I have often seen blues, browns and granams on at the same time, when they have refused the other two sorts, and have taken the browns only. There cannot be too much said in commendation of this fly, both for its duration, and the sport he affords the angler: The size of the hook he is made on, is No. 6.

Oh! for the days of such prolific hatches!

The Bowlkers also possessed a good knowledge of fly-tying and in a section entitled 'The Manner of Making the Artificial Fly' give, like Barker, a description of the operations as follows.

When you make an artificial Fly, you must, in the first place, make choice of a hook of a size proportionable to the Fly you intend to make, which must be whipped on to your gut or hair in the same manner you would whip on a worm-hook, only with this difference, that instead of fastening near the bend of the hook, you must fasten your silk near the top of the shank, and let your silk remain; then taking as much feather as is necessary for the wings, lay it as even as you can upon the upper side of the shank, with the but end of the feather downward, towards the bend of the hook, and tye it fast three or four times with the silk and fasten it; then, with a needle or pin, divide the wings as equal as you can; then take your silk and cross it three or four times between the wings, bringing the silk still downward, towards the bend of the hook, then taking your hackle feather, tye it fast at the bend with the point of the hackle upwards; next, your fur or dubbing being ready, which is to make the body of the Fly, take a little of it and twist it gently round your silk, and work it upwards to the but of the wings, and there fasten it; then take your hackle and rib it neatly over your dubbing, and fasten it; then bending the wings and putting them into the form you design, bring on the but end of your hackle towards the head, and there fasten it firm; then taking a bit of dubbing or fur, as near to the colour of the head of the Fly as you can, whip it twice or thrice round with your silk, and then fasten it just above the wings; so your Fly is completed.

Where the Bowlkers' detail is more advanced is shown in their attempts to copy the natural fly giving greater attention to shape, form, colour and hue, coupled with an appreciation of the hook sizes needed and which they specify – something I have not seen in any of the earlier fly-dressing patterns. They disposed of the patterns of the 'Treatyse' and substituted a more modern list considerably more practical because the flies were evolved by anglers with at least some knowledge of entomology.

In later editions of the book it is the son, Charles Bowlker, who is shown as the author, a fly-fisherman more advanced than any other of his time.

Then, in 1800, came the first book to provide additional guidance by way of illustrations of natural insects in colour. This was *The Fly-Fisher's Legacy* by George Scotcher and other new ground was broken since he refers to the use of a floating fly.

A few years later, in 1816, appeared *The Fly-Fisher's Guide* by George Bainbridge, this also providing colour illustrations of natural insects but in greater number, covering five plates.

James Tod Stoddart's *The Art of Angling as Practised in Scotland* appeared in 1835. Stoddart practised the art of the wet fly, a subject about which he wrote with absolute authority.

Each new publication indicates a widening entomological knowledge, but the landmark appeared in 1836 when, in London, came the publication of *The Fly Fisher's Entomology* by Alfred Ronalds containing colour illustrations of an exceedingly high standard. This work is entirely original and combines the knowledge of a seasoned angler with the observant eye of the keen naturalist, the perfect combination to produce this classic guide which, from that day forward, has set a standard few others have attained. As an example of the thoroughness of his observations I give his detail for 'No. 16 Iron Blue Dun.'

No. 16.   Iron Blue Dun

After emerging from its water nympha, this fly remains about two days in the state shewn, and then changes to the Jenny Spinner . . . It is one of the smallest flies worth the Angler's notice, but not the least useful. The male has a brownish red crown or cap on his head. The female is also crowned, but her cap is too small to be easily seen. It is in season from the latter end of April until the middle of June, and is on the water chiefly on cold days; influenced by effects similar to those which act upon the Blue Dun . . .

Imitation

Body.   Blue fur from a mole. A little reddish brown floss silk may be tied on with dun silk for the head.

Tail.   A whisk or two out of a dun hackle.

Wings.   From a feather of the underside of the cormorant's wing; but as this bird is scarce, and has only a few feathers under the wing, a very good substitute may be found in a feather from the breast of the water hen; the tip of which must be used.

Legs.   A very useful small dun hackle, or some of the dubbing picked out of the body.

It is difficult to find a hackle feather of the tint proper to make this fly buzz.

A subsequent edition of Ronalds' work, dated 1913 and limited to 250 copies, included an enlightening innovation. Forty-eight specimen flies in sunken mounts are provided in addition to the excellent hand-coloured plates, the whole combining to provide a first-class reference.

The nineteenth century proved to be a period in which writing on fly-fishing and the art of fly-tying reached new heights and it was an important period in the development of the 'gentle art' albeit mainly confined to the wet fly. However, the more discerning of those who practised this form of fishing observed that the trout would rise to a fly which, probably due to handling or an excess of materials in the making, or both, floated for a short period although designed and dressed as a wet fly. This is borne out by the observations of G. P. R. Pulman in *The Vade-Mecum of Fly-*

Fishing for Trout of 1841 in which he refers to intentional false casting to dry a fly, almost certainly a wet pattern, to be offered as a floater to trout feeding on the surface.

In 1853 Michael Theakston's *A List of Natural Flies* was published. This work had much to recommend it but, regretably, it departed from the orthodox in the nomenclature. Nevertheless, it was well received and certainly added to the growing body of knowledge on the subject.

W. H. Aldam followed Ronalds' example by including in his *A Quaint Treatise on Flees, and the Art a Artyfichall Flee Making* (1876) 25 artificial flies in sunken mounts which are a delight in themselves. The mounts include the actual materials used – a particulary valuable guide. It is a little difficult to read because of the artificially quaint and, at times, comical phraseology, for instance,

> When you have made a Artifichall flee as nate as hand can make It is a thousand times behind a natural one when dresst with the natest meatearills –When wee come to Examin thoes small beautyfull tender dellagate and nate water bred Duns that ought to be the Anglers coppiing – I can find no room for coace meatearills – the natest are very coace when compared.

This Adam says, comes from a manuscript which was written 'by an old man well known on the Derbyshire streams as a first class fly fisher.' Aldam's book provides an excellent guide of a kind not often met with because of the cost involved in the inclusion of the flies and materials. Such riches are not common in angling literature and then only in limited editions of which this was one, only 100 copies being produced.

The introduction of the so-called 'dry' fly specifically designed not only in size, form and colour as a representation of the natural fly, but also with the precise intention that it should *float on the surface* in a natural way, followed the elaboration of his invention, the snecky Limerick eyed-hook, by H. S. Hall, c. 1879, following the earlier unsuccessful attempts by Hewett Wheatly in 1849 to produce such hooks.

The cult of the dry fly developed on the chalk streams of the south of England where fly life was prolific and surface feeding on duns and spinners could frequently be observed. No doubt isolated anglers were formulating their own theories concerning the efficacy of floating flies but it was Frederic Michael Halford who established a methodical approach, basing his studies on the precise representation of natural insects which formed the food of the trout. Halford's *Floating Flies and how to dress them* appeared in 1886, fulfilling a need for guidance on the design and use of the dry fly. In his researches his close friend George Selwyn Marryat, regarded by many as the finest fly-fisherman of the time, gave practical guidance and assistance based on his own wide experience and it is a very great pity that he never published a book of his own. Being a perfectionist, Halford went to great lengths in producing accurate copies of the insects and was in the forefront of the development of a method of winging the flies to avoid the earlier fault which caused the fly to spin when being cast. The spin arose from the use of slips of feather taken from *the same quill*. This caused the wing tips to lean to one side and to function in the manner of a propeller blade under wind pressure. This put a twist in the leader and tended to retard the forward motion of the fly.

Halford, inspired by Hall, and particularly by Marryat the inventive genius, revised fly design by using slips from quills on opposing wings which avoided the problem of spin and also enabled the fly to cock properly and sit upright on the water in a realistic manner. Changes made in body materials which aided floatation and the use of really high quality capes to provide hackles and whisks applied to Hall's new eyed hook helped to establish the dry fly, the use of which was largely made possible by the invention of the oiled silk line. All this inspired a school of thought which held that the floating fly must rule supreme. This view Halford held so firmly that, subsequently, his prejudice bordered on bigotry and was reflected in his writing.

Halford was meticulous and painstaking in his efforts to achieve the exact representation of the natural fly. In *Modern Development of the Dry Fly* (1910) he defined his range of colours and shades by numbers so that each subtle hue of wing, body, legs and whisks could be precisely matched although in the seven books that he published there is not a single colour illustration of a natural fly and the reader is, therefore, required to have blind faith in Halford's definition of the colours of the live insects which, for study, he immersed in preservative, a process which so often produces colour changes. He was not a wet fly man and did not understand the practice. As time went on he developed a hostility to the use of the wet fly on chalk streams (which he called 'dry-fly streams') and, according to the need of the argument, referred to the use of the wet fly as 'unfruitful, positively harmful, or illegitimate.'

What Halford did was to design his flies round the new eyed hook. He omitted the gut and its necessary whipping from beneath the body material which he changed from dubbing to quill. Thus the fly was that much lighter in weight and floated better, the gut then being joined to the eye. This had another advantage for, should the gut at the eye show signs of weakening, it was a simple task to cut out the weak portion and *retie the same fly*. In addition, the thickness of the gut to which the fly, on an eyed hook, is joined can be changed at will whereas when the gut was built into the body on a blind hook this was not possible, the fly necessarily being either thrown away or becoming one of a sort of nostalgic collection at home.

A great deal of the development of the dry fly as we know it today is due to the trio, Hall, Halford and Marryat, but it was Halford in his direct style who produced, particularly in *Dry Fly Fishing in Theory and Practice* (1889), the angling literature destined to bring to the angling world a most comprehensive dry fly code for chalk streams and he was undoubtedly the finest angling writer of his time. His contribution must be recognised as the result of years of intelligent and unstinting study. It must be a matter of regret, however, that *The Dry-fly Man's Handbook* of 1913 was so dedicated to dry fly purism that the use of the wet fly became a sort of heresy and this narrowness of outlook brought him into conflict with those holding a more balanced view, doing nothing to improve his reputation but rather the reverse.

In 1886 T. E. Pritt's *North-Country Flies* was also published. This was a de-luxe edition of *Yorkshire Trout Flies* published the year before. It records many of the old north country favourites in addition to others exemplifying the hackled fly with sparse dressing, devoid of all glittery tinsel or dressy materials. This style is still popular, particularly in the north. In addition, he provides 62 hand-painted illustrations of wet fly patterns in 11 plates for guidance.

The last, but by no means the least, of the publications of interest produced in the nineteenth century was a work, small only in size, by Harry G. McClelland, first published in 1898 called *How to Tie Flies for Trout and Grayling* which, due to the excellence of the contents, ran to ten editions, the last of which appeared as recently as 1949. Harry McClelland was already well known for his articles which appeared in *Fishing Gazette* under the name 'Athenian' and these were considered of such value that the *Gazette* gathered them into book form. Apart from expressing his view that exact imitation should be the aim, he gives a wealth of information on materials, their preparation including the dyeing processes, and the various operations necessary to incorporate them to the best advantage. The drawings, which accompany the text, amplify so well what he writes, that it is no wonder that, in its useful pocket book size it was, as the number of editions proclaims, a very popular work. Alas, illness is no respecter of persons, and he died at an early age. I am sure that, had he lived, his pen would have produced further works of value to us.

Then, in 1910, to take up the cudgels on behalf of the wet fly came George Edward Mackenzie Skues with *Minor Tactics of the Chalk Stream*. There is nothing 'minor' about Skues' work. He writes with great simplicity and conviction, clearly disliking the continuation of customs and traditions which have lost their meaning. The wet fly having virtually been banished from the Itchen, he reasons with and cajoles the reader to consider that if the wet fly had been successful before the advent of the dry fly, was not there room for it still? He brought to his aid a series of experiments designed to convince the doubtful and he fought prejudice with facts using, for instance, the post mortem examination of the fly life in a trout's stomach to support his views. He set to work to redesign the wet fly including new nymph-suggesting patterns turning for inspiration, somewhat surprisingly, to the flies of the Clyde and the Tweed.

Outside southern England the wet fly in general still held pride of place but the floating fly was coming more into use, although complementary to the wet fly rather than in place of it. Skues, refusing to be borne along with the dry-fly-only tide, and finding no sensible justification for the rejection of the wet fly which had not been discredited but simply ostracised on the chalk streams he had fished for so long, set about producing his case for the effectiveness and suitability of the wet fly. As one would expect from a member of the legal profession, he used his vast experience, subtle and lucid argument and convincing experiment so persuasively and with such authority that not only has *Minor Tactics* become a classic but his work has not since been seriously challenged. Side by side with his arguments Skues developed and produced a series of representations of various species of natural nymphs which, by their very success in the face of quite formidable opposition from the dry fly school of thought, helped to re-establish acceptance of the wet fly in its various forms on his beloved streams.

Subsequently, in his second major contribution, *The Way of a Trout with a Fly* (1921), he set out to improve upon former wet fly design and gives practical and constructive guidance to fly-dressers and fly-fishermen helpful not only on chalk streams but also on rough and tumbling streams elsewhere. *Nymph Fishing for Chalk Stream Trout* appeared in 1939, a further substantial contribution dealing as it does with a series of representations of natural nymphs. This book was the result of long study and observation coupled with a significant ability to transpose shape, form and colour into the artificial patterns he devised. This was a peak in fly-dressing art. Any fly-fisherman or fly-dresser seeking a greater understanding of trout and fly life will find Skues' books deal with the subjects logically and liberally and much will be gained in the reading.

Skues is also well known for the articles he produced for *Fishing Gazette,* for many years the leading angling journal, alas, no longer published. He wrote under the pseudonym of 'Val Conson' and the articles which referred to fly-dressing or, rather, fly-tying as it was becoming called, were published as a pocket-sized book in 1950 under the title *Silk, Fur and Feather* which has much to offer the beginner as well as the more experienced fly-tyer. The book is in ten parts, dealing with various aspects of the trout fly-fisher's year but a separate un-numbered section at the end, comprising 27 pages, is devoted to and entitled *The Fly-*

Dresser's Birds which is quite enlightening although the plumage of some of the birds referred to has now either gone out of favour or is unobtainable. A useful guide in many ways, nevertheless.

Skues pointed the way in the useful study of natural fly life and others followed, one such being Leonard West whose book, privately published in 1912, entitled *The Natural Trout Fly and its Imitation* deals with the identification and representation of various species of insects which form the food of trout, amplified by plates in colour of natural and artificial flies and similar plates of feathers and hackles used in tying the patterns.

There followed, in 1921, the work of Martin E. Mosely. *The Dry-Fly Fisherman's Entomology* is small in size but certainly not in scope, obviously intended to be carried in the pocket whilst angling. Mosely was an entomologist in the Department of Entomology of the British Museum (Natural History) for over 20 years. In the Museum there is a wonderful collection of his preserved natural specimens, many of which are described in his book and superbly illustrated in colour. It is a book written from an expert point of view and is of great value to the fly-fisherman with an interest in entomology.

Mosely was a nephew of Halford and shortly before his death in 1948 bequeathed to the Museum one of the few un-numbered copies of the de-luxe first edition of Halford's *Modern Development of the Dry Fly* (1910). This comprises two volumes, the second of which contains 33 of Halford's patterns in sunken mounts, some dressed by Hardy Bros Ltd, of Alnwick, and others by C. Farlow & Co. This presentation copy is inscribed 'Martin E. Mosely, Esq., with kindest regards and many thanks from Frederic M. Halford,' perhaps in acknowledgment of his nephew's advice. This copy, together with editions of most, if not all, of Halford's other works, can be seen by arrangement in the Entomology Library of the British Museum.

The search for methods of closely representing natural insects was carried further by J. W. Dunne who, in 1924, produced his book *Sunshine and the Dry Fly*. Dunne was absorbed in attempts to reproduce, using artificial means, the translucency and colouration of insects as they appeared in various conditions of light, including the strength and angle of the source – the sun. His experiments led him to the discovery that if the shank of the hook were to be painted white to provide reflection of light, and the body of the fly formed over it by winding on *artificial* silk (cellulite), an application of colourless paraffin applied and absorbed could then produce a superbly translucent body without any sign of the metal hook shank showing through, *but* that translucency would only be produced in conditions of bright light or sunshine – therein lay the problem. Nevertheless, Dunne was sufficiently confident to produce over 30 patterns which he considered would be effective given the necessary conditions of light. However, possibly due to scepticism, the complicated body dressings involving the blending of silks of different colours, or because the right conditions of light do not always pertain, his cellulite-bodied flies did not achieve broad acceptance or popularity. All the same, his theories did have merit and it is a little disappointing that no-one else seems to have pursued the possibilities of translucency by some means or other.

A rather wider field is covered in *Modern Trout Fly Dressing* (1932). The author, Roger Woolley, provided descriptions accompanied by colour plates, of a wide range of materials for use in dressings and his coverage must have been some of the best up to that time. There is much helpful advice on how to set about dyeing plumage and other materials for various fly-tying purposes and the methods to be employed in making the best use of their natural shape and characteristics in tying the flies he lists. He covers a wide field, embracing river, lake and sea-trout flies and, what is more, he deals with size, form and colour in the various stages of metamorphosis of the natural fly represented, a definite contribution to the development of the fly-tyer's knowledge.

Taking us further along the road of twentieth-century patterns and processes is *Fly-Tying for Trout* by Eric Taverner, published in 1939. This comprises the fly-tying sections and dressings drawn from an earlier book of his entitled *Trout Fishing from all Angles* which, as the title indicates, covered a very wide field. *Fly-Tying for Trout* incorporates two colour plates, the first showing various types and styles of dressing from different parts of the country comparing the slim and sparse bodies preferred on the Tummel and Clyde and in Yorkshire, to the comparatively flamboyant Mayfly and delicate Olive (Red) Spinner of Halford's south. There is much to be learned of the different approaches made by fly-tyers to cater for the rough and tumbling waters of the north where the wet fly holds reign, to the smooth and clear waters of the chalk streams. The other plate is devoted to hen and cock hackles which were most in demand, as well as examples of spade and saddle feathers suitable for whisks, etc. Whilst the colour reproduction is not to the standard one now expects, the latter plate does provide helpful visual reference for those not well acquainted with the fly-tying terms for these feathers. Equally helpful are the drawings in the latter part of the book and those on page 102 and the accompanying text provide clear instructions on how to produce the 'rolled wing' formed from a section of web from a primary or secondary feather of the starling, for example. As a further aid there is a black and white photograph depicting the outer and inner sides of a snipe's wing, identifying the position of the types of feathers commonly used in fly-dressing. The dressings described are a combination of reliable standard patterns and those of the more well known personalities such as Halford, Marryat, Skues and Austin and the book as a whole takes us one more step in the advancement of our fly-tying knowledge.

In *Fly-tying: Principles and Practice* (1940), Major Gerald Burrard, DSO, RFA (Retd), then Editor of *Game and Gun,* enlarges upon the 'loop' method employed in winging, an operation which can be a trial for the inexperienced, and the 'figure-of-eight' whip for wing security, particularly the 'spent' wing. The drawings which accompany the text are particularly helpful in understanding the problems involved. Then again, his description and illustrations of the whip finish as it is made by hand are clear and concise and the book is well named, not only for those aspects I have mentioned, but because it contains a wealth of other useful hints and tips of interest not only to the beginner but to the more proficient. Winging, bodies of dubbing and quill, ribbing hackles and 'detached' bodies are all dealt with and the addition of dressings for trout and salmon adds to the book's value as a progressive work.

Unfortunately, further development was interrupted by the advent of the Second World War and it is not until 1952 that the next major figure appears.

Who better to advise on materials and fly-tying techniques and processes than John Veniard who possesses a very extensive and special knowledge of plumage and fur resulting from the connection his company had with the fur and millinery trades in earlier years. After the war John's fly-tying and fly-fishing experience was utilised in the business and as an ambassador of the sport he had correspondence with innovators and experimenting fly-tyers all over the world and with many who sought his guidance with their problems. This wealth of knowledge and experience, coupled with his almost unique understanding of the materials associated with fly-tying are revealed in his *Fly-Dresser's Guide* (1952) which has, for many years, been regarded as the standard work on the subject. As one would expect, there is very extensive coverage of materials, their treatment and use, and the text, accompanying drawings and plates in black and white and colour clear away much of the mystique previously associated with fly-tying. This book was a considerable contribution to the growing interest in the subject and was followed by *A Further Guide to Fly-Dressing* (1964) and *Reservior and Lake Flies* (1970).

Meantime, the rapid expansion in the provision of trout fishing on reservoirs and private fisheries increased the demand for tuition in fly-tying and those who could not attend courses held at Adult Education Centres and elsewhere sought to assuage their thirst for knowledge in more and more books of instruction.

John Veniard rose to the occasion and in collaboration with Donald Downs, a superb illustrator, produced *Fly-Tying Problems* (1970) followed two years later by *Fly-Tying Development and Progress* and, in 1977, by *Fly-Dressing Materials* bringing up to date our knowledge on changing styles, revised procedures and new materials.

Whereas Halford had advocated exact representation of the natural fly, others, by personal fishing experience and extensive observation over long periods, developed different theories. One such was Frank Sawyer, Keeper of the Officers' Association water on the Wiltshire Avon who, in 1958, wrote *Nymphs and the Trout,* the main subject of which is nymphs belonging to the active and swimming group, knowledge of which can be put to good and effective use in the deception of trout and other fish provided that, in fashioning one's artificial, account is taken of 'First, the general appearance, shape, colouring and translucency. Secondly, it must be made to enter quickly without any addition afterwards to make it sink. Thirdly, and this is essential, so that it can be cast both accurately and delicately as the occasion demands.' Note that Sawyer uses the word 'general' in his first consideration, not 'exact.' Sawyer designed a number of very effective flies on the basis of these principles, perhaps the most successful and well known being his pheasant tail pattern, Sawyer's Nymph, which has been proved effective throughout the world. Others are Killer Bug, Grey Goose and Bow-tie Buzzer, this last designed for use by lake fishermen mainly on waters where large chironomids, commonly known as buzzers, may be present. Exact representation? Not a bit of it, as can be seen from his Killer Bug pattern, originally intended for grayling but subsequently found effective for reservoir and lake trout. This nymph pattern has a double layer of copper wire wound round the shank over which is then wound a wool/nylon mending yarn generally known as Chadwick's Wool which, for colour, is identified as number 477. The body is produced with a somewhat simple maggot-like shape yet it is very effective due, says Sawyer, to the fact that this particular yarn changes colour completely when wet and is the main cause of its attraction for the fish. This, from a man who spent his life by the water, is different thinking indeed.

So it was with Major Oliver Kite who, until his untimely death in 1969, had established a considerable reputation for his success as a nymph-fisher and now widely known for his 'bare-hook' nymph, a pattern comprising a hump representing the thorax and wing cases built up of fine copper wire wound behind the eye of an otherwise bare hook, though a few fibres from a red/brown pheasant tail feather might be added to provide a slightly hairy appearance – an almost total rejection of exact representation. This nymph also exemplifies the three principles of Sawyer. However, Kite by no means totally rejected representation, for in dry fly fishing he utilised eight or ten patterns, the greater number of which resembled, at least to some extent, the insect on which his quarry was feeding. The art of using patterns of the type designed by Sawyer and Kite lies in ensuring that the fly has sunk to the depth at which the fish is positioned and in the simulation of the movement of the natural nymph. In expert hands this can be devastatingly successful and Major Kite's book *Elements of Nymph Fishing* (1966) is, indeed, interesting and illuminating, coming from a man with an originality of mind and clarity of expression.

W. H. Lawrie, internationally known as an authority on fly patterns, sets down a comprehensive record in the several books he produced between 1966 and 1972 beginning with *Scottish Trout Flies* which deals with those of the Tummel, Tweed and Clyde as well as the lochs. Then, in 1967, came three books in rapid succession – *English and Welsh Trout Flies, All Fur Flies and How to Dress Them,* the latter bringing attention to the greater use of hair for wings and tails and fur for bodies, and *A Reference Book of English Trout Flies,* a work describing dressings from the time of the 'Treatyse' of 1496. This book covers the major works of Bowlker, Ronalds, Pritt, Halford, Woolley and many others – a fascinating study of evolution. His *International Trout Flies* appeared in 1969 and is a work which enables one to compare the fly-tying styles of France, Italy, the United States, Canada, Australasia and elsewhere, with those of the United Kingdom. For the Richard Walker Library, Lawrie produced *Modern Trout Flies* (1972) dealing with patterns for the south, west and north of England and the Border areas. It deals with nymphs, wet and dry flies for trout and grayling as well as lures for reservoirs. There is much to be learned from all Lawrie's works which are worth a place on any angler's bookshelves.

Where other writers dealt mainly with patterns, materials or techniques, John Goddard concentrates essentially on the entomological aspect of the subject. In 1966 his *Trout Fly Recognition* appeared, dealing with the identification of various species of river-bred flies and, in 1969, he published *Trout Flies of Still Water* which deals with flies of lake and reservoir. Both books are the result of extensive research and include many colour plates of duns, spinners, nymphs and other insects which Goddard photographed himself, a task involving immense patience.

Gone are the days when we had to rely on written descriptions or hand-coloured plates, beautiful as they might be. Here is the photographic evidence, in colour, of the shape, size and form, accompanied by details of the habitat, life cycle, distribution and time of emergence of many of the insects of interest to the angler. If one desires to match the hatch this work provides the detail. In both books there are dressings by the author and other accomplished fly-dressers, amplified by photographs of the completed flies. Prodigious works both.

In conjuction with Brian Clarke, whose own book *The Pursuit of Still-*

water Trout aroused such interest when it appeared in 1978, John Goddard pursued his researches. The result of this collaboration is *The Trout and the Fly* (1980) which includes new patterns based on their studies of the 'cone of vision' of the trout and its 'window' to the sky. Their observations gave them a clear insight into what the fish first sees and how it then recognises the duns and spinners on the surface which are carried into its vision by the flow of the current. The 'cone of vision' and 'window' (see fig. 2) have been referred to by earlier writers, among them Taverner in *Trout Fishing from all Angles,* Vincent C. Marinaro in *A Modern Dry Fly Code* (1950) and Skues who discusses it in *The Way of a Trout with a Fly.*

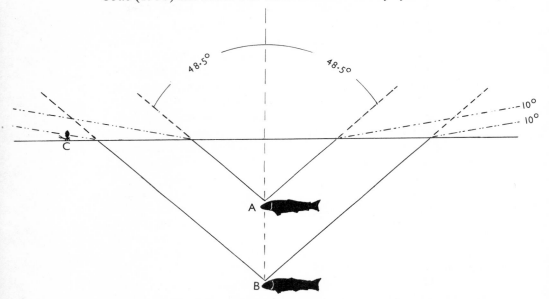

2   *The cone of vision for both trout in the diagram is 97°, that is, 48.5° on either side of the perpendicular. A circle on the surface bounded by the edge of the cone is called the trout's 'window,' the size of which increases in relation to the depth at which the fish lies, thus the 'window' for trout 'A' is smaller than that for trout 'B.' The under-surface of the water* outside *the cone of vision acts as a mirror reflecting underwater objects and fish are unable to see through it. Refraction bends the edge of the cone above the surface down to the lowest angle at which light can penetrate, that is approximately 10°. Trout 'B' can, therefore, see the wings of the fly 'C' which break through his 10° line, but they are not visible to trout 'A' because they are below his 10° line.*

Using underwater photography, Clarke and Goddard confirmed that the first indication a fish lying in the stream has that a fly is approaching on the surface is the pin-points of light caused by the legs of the fly making small depressions in the suface of the 'mirror' outside the 'cone of vision.'

As the fly proceeds downstream with the flow of the current and approaches, but before it enters the 'window,' the upper tips of the wing are seen. The nearer the fly approaches the 'window' the more the fish sees of the fly until, when it is carried into the edge of the 'window' the whole of the fly becomes clearly visible to the fish. If the current is fairly fast flowing the fish has little time to make its observations and assessment but, in this connection, Marinaro, in *A Modern Dry Fly Code* tells of an experiment carried out in the United States in which Mr James Kell, at the height of a hatch on a water known as Yellow Beeches, caught a number of up-winged duns and removed the wings. The hatch was heavy and the winged duns were readily being taken by the rising fish. Mr Kell then intermittently floated his wingless flies downstream to the fish which continued to rise and take the winged creatures but *not one of the wingless specimens.* This experiment, whilst by no means conclusive, would seem to support the theory that if the fish does not see in an approaching fly the points of recognition it looks for, it may shun it. It could be this process which enables the fish to select flies of which it is particularly fond as food, say the Blue Winged Olive, from a hatch composed of a number of different flies, Iron Blues, Pale Wateries, Blue Winged Olives and Large Dark Olives, for instance. Perhaps the fish's reactions go like this as the various types appear – 'the wings of that one are too tall,' or 'that's not what I'm looking for because the wings are too light in colour.' Of course, it might just as easily react, when an angler's newly created artificial appears: 'Hullo, that's new; orange wings and fifteen bright green legs – I wonder what it is and what it tastes like.' Or, just as likely, 'Some chap must think I'm stupid.' Nevertheless, whatever it might or might not be considering, the fish is *using the points of recognition* in deciding to take, or not to take, the offering. Clarke and Goddard have developed dun and spinner patterns which are tied with the hook point upside down, i.e., above the surface rather than below it. It is interesting that R. B. Marston, onetime editor of *Fishing Gazette* was producing patterns with the hook point upside down in the 1880s but they did not receive wide recognition. In standard patterns the hook point is below the dressing and, therefore, normally penetrates the surface film. The advantage of the hook point upside down is that there is no penetration of the surface – the 'mirror' – as the fly approaches the fish and thus one of the possible causes of rejection of the fly with the hook point down may have been overcome.

In colour photograph 48 and the drawings on page 165 of USD Para-Olive you will see that their design has wings produced by a 'wing cutter' tool. Stuart Canham, a superb fly-tyer, who tied many of the specimen models during the stages of development of the Clarke/Goddard flies, was making prototypes of these cutters when he was a member of my fly-tying class in the early 1970s and many were the variations he and a colleague produced at that time from bits of razor blade affixed in a wooden handle. His commercially produced sets of wing cutters are now widely used. However, to revert to the design. The usual form of hackle wound round the hook shank has not been used but, instead, a hackle horizontally wound in 'Parachute' style, a name and method patented by Alexander Martin of Glasgow in 1933. However, where Martin's hackles were above, Clarke and Goddard's are below the body. What their patterns set out to accomplish are dry flies which sit *wholly* on or only just above the water, nothing projecting below, and although up-eyed hooks are used, remember that the dressing is tied upside down, as follows.

3   USD Para-Olive

Whether the type and shape of wings used, together with the 'Parachute' style of hackle, will counterbalance the weight of that part of the hook pointing upward and so permit, or rather ensure, that the fly consistently will settle on the surface *right way up* may appear doubtful but the authors maintain that in the tests they have carried out the ratio works out at better than 80 per cent in favour of it doing so. Inevitably, the radical change from hook point down to hook point up will start a chain of thought. For instance –

Will there be less chance of hooking securely if the point, assuming it is upward at the take, is towards the more bony part of the fish's mouth? Is there not an equal chance that the fly will land on its side, that is, standing on the points of wing and hackle? If it does land on its side, the tip of the wing usually seen in the vertical position will not appear to provide the recognition point for the fish and the fly may be ignored as were the 'wingless' flies mentioned by Marinaro. The use of hackle fibres to represent the legs of the fly and the type of wing may still be found to have the same weakness as some of the conventional patterns which pose problems of collapsibility. If one takes the surface of the water as the median line, the fish will rise from below it and, in the conventional fly the hook point is more or less pointing down toward the fish, whereas in the hook up patterns one has to rely on the sip or suck by the fish to bring the fly and the point down and into its mouth. In practice, there may well be no difference in the hooking capability .

I have dealt with Clarke and Goddard's developments at some length since that which they advocate as a result of their observation and experiment seems to be a distinct departure from the line of evolution of the trout fly as we have known it to date. One thing is certain. As the many other writers mentioned herein have in their own way contributed to the evolution of the patterns generally accepted today, so this research has moved fly design one stage further and it is intriguing to consider what new patterns may emerge from this approach.

Of the various books mentioned in these pages many, alas, are out of print and thus not only scarce but very expensive if they can be found. There are several booksellers specialising in old and new angling literature and quite a number of volumes can be borrowed through the public library system. Occasionally a gem can be found among the motley collections in the charity shops, jumble sales and other unlikely places. To my everlasting regret, I missed a rare and valuable copy of William Scrope's *Days and Nights of Salmon Fishing in the Tweed* (1843) which was at the bottom of a box of assorted thrillers and romances in a country market auction, because I went for a cup of coffee at the wrong time!

I must not convey the impression that innovation in trout fly design is confined to the United Kingdom, for this is far from true. Trout fishing has long been a popular sport in many countries. In the United States the sheer size and spread of the population has inevitably produced a wide range of new thinking and new patterns to meet the requirements of anglers fishing a great variety of waters. This has resulted in radical changes in what had previously been mainly British patterns. We find, for instance, that flies in use on waters in the Catskills differ in many respects from those for Pennsylvania.

One of the earlier men of note was Theodore Gordon (1854–1915) whose popular Quill Gordon pattern used wood duck for the wing as did the Light and Dark Cahills developed by Daniel Cahill, and the Hendrickson patterns. These dressings must have taken countless fish at the height of their popularity and they are still in use today.

It was inevitable that differing styles of fly-tying would develop in areas far apart so that in travelling the country one would find as much diversity of pattern as if one visited foreign lands although some standard patterns, or slight variants, were universally popular, at least for a time. One such variation was the Bi-visible. This used two hackles at the head of the fly and Edward R. Hewitt is credited with popularising it in the 1890s. His patterns specified the use of a white hackle to be wound on immediately behind the eye, a darker hackle then being wound palmerwise over the rest of the shank. Later, Peter Schwab, a West Coast fishing expert, introduced bright orange or yellow to replace the white, this change being based on US Army and Navy research on colours, their attraction for fish and the visibility of such colours at a distance.

Another interesting development was the use of bucktail fibres spun round the hook shank and clipped to shape to form a body. An example of this is Rat-Faced McDougal, a fly with excellent floating properties.

Lee Wulff's series of the 1930s blazed a new trail by utilising fur and hair for body and wings respectively. His patterns had enormous success and sparked off a wave of interest in the use of these materials for fly-tying, a use now firmly established.

Later, dry flies came to be dressed with longer and stiffer hackles and these were set further back from the hook eye than is commonly seen in the United Kingdom, the intention being to create a better balanced fly, more support being given to the bend where lies the heavier weight, the longer, stiffer hackle enabling the fly to ride high on the water. The only drawback was the reduced distance such flies could be cast due to the increased wind resistance of the greater spread of hackle, although it must be admitted that they alighted like gossamer.

In the 1950s Vincent Marinaro propounded many theories on fly design among which were the use of porcupine quills with which to form detached bodies and hackles cut to shape to form wings similar to the USD Paraduns of Clarke and Goddard.

At about this time wings seem to have lost much of their attraction and hackled flies came to the fore. Where wings were used these were of the 'bunched' wing type, bunches of fibres stripped from a hackle and tied in upright as a single wing or divided, both styles appearing less opaque, when viewed against the light, than solid fibre wings from duck or starling. Later, hackleless flies were introduced, the fly body being designed to provide all the necessary floatation although wings were still incorporated, a design by Doug Swisher and Carl Richards.

Another development came from Frank Johnson of Missoula, Montana, whose 'Waterwalkers' involved the use of two hackles, one wound diagonally round each half of a divided wing. An apt name for these high riding flies.

Much has been written elsewhere on the American point of view and I have included in the bibliography notable titles which may be of interest.

Elsewhere in the world devotees of trout fishing have designed patterns suitable for their own waters. In France, a country abounding in first-rate fly-fishing, the sport flourishes. On the subject of *mouches artificielles* the anglers are knowledgeable and skilled craftsmen, particularly in the design and, may I add, the use of the dry fly. There appears to be less interest in wings of solid fibre; hackled patterns are to the fore with wings of hackle tips tied upright, 'spent' or forward over the eye as in our Mole Fly.

In Germany where the quality of the sport is maintained at a high standard and greatly esteemed, a number of British patterns are favoured as are those of France, although a little larger in size than one would expect for use on alpine streams. Some Italian patterns, generally more petite, are also in favour in Germany and, particularly, in Austria.

In Italy, wet patterns predominate and are mainly of the hackled variety usually dressed to a high standard. Greater use is made of fluorescent material, particularly for tags and to accentuate the head of the fly.

On the waters of Switzerland and Yugoslavia many Italian patterns are favoured as well as some of the hackled patterns of France.

In New Zealand, with its magnificent trout waters, many British patterns or variants are still in use but many localised patterns have evolved. One such is the Matuka, a corruption of *matuku,* the Maori word for the bittern, feathers from which originally provided wings for lures but, since the bird is now protected, other plumage has replaced it. The names applied to some flies indicate their origin; thus the Taupo Tiger and the Tiahape Tickler. These and a great many more are recorded by Keith Draper in his *Trout Flies of New Zealand* (1971), a most informative work for this area.

Australian flies include, not surprisingly, a number of New Zealand patterns but British flies are particularly in evidence in Tasmania where cooler conditions foster more abundant fly life, encouraging the interest in fly-fishing there. Elsewhere, varying altitudes and temperatures limit natural fly life and beetle patterns are more in evidence.

It is inevitable that patterns to suit a particular locality will continue to evolve. This is part of the interest and challenge of fly-tying. I have little doubt that at this moment in many parts of the world fly-tyers are busy with their own ideas and on variations of old favourites, all directed to deceiving the trout.

Foreign travel, simplified by modern air routes, has greatly encouraged the interchange of information and I foresee that in the not too distant future every travelling fly-fisherman will carry a selection of patterns suitable for any water in a couple of flyboxes.

We cannot, even if we wished to, halt the evolution of the trout fly. My only hope is that the perfect fly which all fish will accept any time it is offered will never be devised, for if it were, our pleasure in travelling hopefully would be gone forever. Inspiration – sure; innovation – fine; perfection – never!

2

Tools and Materials

In earlier times the selection of fly-tying materials was much more limited than it is today. Dame Juliana, Izaak Walton and their successors would have used wool ('wull'), silk ('cruell'), silver or gold thread or twist, natural hair from bear, cattle and horses, and fur from rabbit, hare (body, mask and ears), ferret, fox and badger. Plumage came from partridge, mallard, snipe, woodcock, coot, moorhen, blackbird, thrush ('throstle'), tom-tit, grouse, common pheasant and starling ('shepstare').

During the nineteenth century the demands of the costume and millinery trades resulted in the importation of more and more exotic plumage, particularly ostrich, golden and silver pheasant, turkey, lyre bird, humming bird, toucan, ibis, crane, stork, kingfisher and, in fact, any feathers decorative or colourful. Those which were decorative but not colourful enough were soon subjected to the dye bath, for instance ostrich plumes. Fur was also in demand, for example silver fox, mink, beaver (for hats), antelope, leopard and others.

This wide range of tempting plumage and fur inevitably drew the attention of fly-tyers, or fly-dressers as they were then called, until today there is hardly any plumage which has not been experimented with. Even budgerigar body feathers make nice wings and spider hackles, and if the dodo bird were still available its plumage would also be plundered. Fur or hair is now used from elk, moose, monkey, grizzly bear, caribou, coyote, deer, ermine (body and tails), kangaroo, lynx, muskrat, oppossum, otter, peccary, racoon, skunk, ringcat, weasel, wolf, woodchuck, and it doesn't stop there. I have tied flies using hair from blondes and brunettes.

Initially, the selection of tools and materials is beset with the problem that if one reads the catalogues provided by suppliers, there is a tendency to be overwhelmed by the wide range offered. Materials come in a vast range of colours and kinds and the variety of tools increases year by year. For running waters the basic requirements will differ from those for lakes and reservoirs. On the former the wet flies used will generally be smaller and more sparsely dressed than those for the latter and the dry fly will be used to a greater degree.

A beginner should not fall into the trap of attempting to provide him-

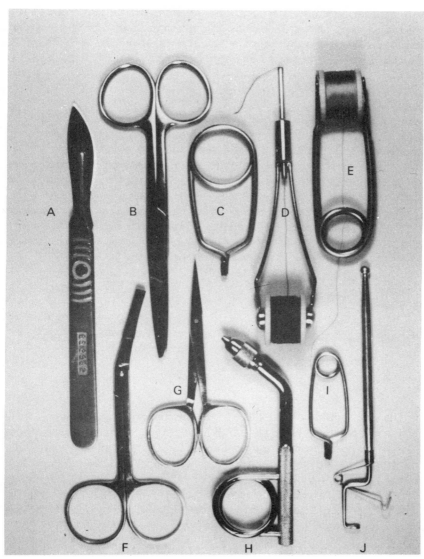

4

A Scalpel with replaceable blades
C Medium hackle pliers
E Standard bobbin holder
  (Veniard's)
G Straight fly-tying scissors
  (fine points)
I Miniature hackle pliers

B Scissors for tinsels and wires
D Spigot-type bobbin holder
F Bent fly-tying scissors
  (fine points)
H Veniard's 'Croydon' hand vice
J Whip finish tool

self with an all-embracing kit; better to limit the initial choice to the essential tools, accompanied by enough materials for a reasonable number of patterns suitable for the waters ordinarily to be visited. Further items can be added as required later.

Tools

Unless you choose to tie your flies using your fingers as a vice like the well-known Michael Rogan of Ballyshannon, County Donegal, Republic of Ireland, and his father, you will need a vice to hold the hook so that both hands are free to manipulate the materials. Bearing in mind that you may, later on, turn to lures or salmon flies with are tied on larger hooks than wet and dry flies, let us begin with the vice.

There are many good models on the market but the choice does not depend on price alone. Manipulation of small flies between the fingers will be found rather difficult in a vice with bulky jaws. In fig. 5, jaws of shape 'A' are preferable to those of shape 'B.'

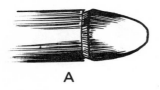 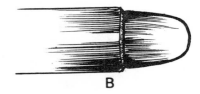

A   B

5   *Vice jaws*

The vice should be adjustable for height and angle and possess a head which will rotate. If large and small hooks are to be handled, remember that it is expecting rather much of a vice to cater for hooks for small dry flies which may be only a quarter of an inch long as well as long-shank lure hooks of up to an inch and a quarter or more. Salmon hooks, or irons as they are called, can be longer still and much thicker in the diameter of the wire. Of the vices I have used over the years my choice would fall on one of the following.

Veniard's *Cranbrook*   A reasonably priced tool. Lever action operates the collet type jaws which are similar in shape to 'A.' It is adjustable for height but not for angle.
Veniard's *Salmo*   Again with jaws as in 'A' but operated by a rotary screw. It has a facility to rotate the jaws round 360° and is also adjustable for height and angle.
Thompson 'A'   With jaws between shape 'A' and 'B.' No rotating action but adjustable for height and angle.

For waterside use the Croydon, which is a hand vice with a collet-type chuck, will be found useful. It is suitable for hooks up to size 10. Also from Veniard.

You will also need –

A pair of sharp, fine-pointed scissors of good quality and with finger holes of adequate size – this latter is important. Keep the points protected in a plastic tube when the scissors are not in use. A pair of medium-size hackle pliers used to wind the hackle round the shank. A pair of miniature hackle pliers will be found useful for the smallest hackles but can be bought later. A pair of stronger-bladed scissors for cutting wires and tinsels for which purpose the scissors mentioned earlier should never be used. A dubbing needle for picking out some of the fibres of a fur body – on Gold Ribbed Hare's Ear, for example. At a pinch this can be a needle firmly glued into a small handle. To have two is best, one for picking out, the other for applying varnish to the head of the fly. A bobbin holder in which to place the spool of tying silk or nylon. Several types are available but cheap plastic versions are best avoided in my opinion although many people use them. The two most in use are Veniard's standard bobbin holder of this shape (fig. 6) and the spigot bobbin holder (fig. 7).

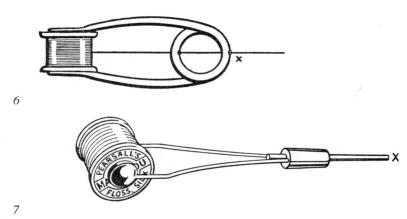

6

7

The American chase bobbin, a spigot type but not freely available in the United Kingdom, is another. One should ensure that the exit area 'X' for the silk or nylon is smooth and will not cause fraying of the material used. This is a fault in some types of bobbin holder. All three mentioned above fit the hand and are efficient. I use both types with equal ease but some tyers find the spigot type more precise in placing the turns of silk. I suppose it really comes down to familiarity with the tool selected. Whilst not essential, a razor blade or better still, a scalpel, is useful for cutting and shaping.

Miscellaneous Aids

Midge Vice Heads
These are miniature vice heads designed to fit into the jaws of the standard vice. Thus, if the jaws of your vice are too bulky to enable you to deal with small hooks down to size 26, a midge head is a useful supplementary tool.

Hackle Guard
For the novice this little aid may avoid spoiling a perfect fly. Basically, a hackle guard is a disk with a central hole. It fits over the eye of the hook and presses the hackle out of the way whilst the head is varnished. Various types are manufactured but at a pinch a coffee stirring stick, which is commonly of flat plastic in the business end of which are holes of various sizes, will suffice, or even a piece of card with a small hole punched in it.

Tweezers
If you buy a pair of tweezers, buy good ones. Too often one finds the points will not firmly grasp what is needed or that one leg is off centre. Of their many uses, one is to pull a hackle tip through a nylon loop when winding 'Parachute' hackles. See *USD Poly-Red Spinner*.

Winging Pliers
Again perhaps useful for the novice, this tool grasps a pair of wings and they are then held in position over the hook shank whilst the tying-in operation is performed.

Matched Wing Pre-selector
This gadget can be adjusted to select almost any fixed width of wing from matched pairs of primary or secondary feathers. It does away with guess-work so often resulting in wings of unequal width.

Whip Finish Tool
This is a mechanical aid which many people feel can accomplish the whip finish more quickly and more precisely than can the human hand. I remember the old saying about 'fingers were made before forks' and finish by hand, but you have the choice.

Gallows Tool
As far as I know, there is only one type, that devised by Bob Barlow. It is used for holding, in tension, the nylon loop employed in tying the 'Parachute' (horizontal) type of hackle. It is fitted to the vice stem and is adjustable for height.

Wing Cutters
This razor-sharp device will cut wings of a predetermined shape from feathers but leaves the lower central quill untouched for use when tying in.

Material Clip
Most vices have a built-in clip intended to secure silk or other material whilst some other operation is performed. However, there is a separate form of clip available which snaps on to the vice post and, unlike that on a vice, is adjustable for height or angle. I cannot remember, in nearly 30 years of fly-tying, ever having felt a need for either.

Hook Point Honing Stone
It is the hook point which secures the fish. A rub with a fine grain stone will make a hook point really sharp.

Magnet
If ever you drop a box of hooks you will learn the advantage of having a magnet to hand. A lost hook may be found at a later date by painful experience.

Vice Base Sheet
I strongly recommend that the area on the table, desk, etc., where you tie your flies be covered with a light coloured paper or cloth. At worst, a sheet of A4 white paper tucked underneath the vice will throw the fly into relief. Try it.

Hooks

Hooks are of by no means recent origin and many specimens of man's ingenuity in this field have been discovered in countries far apart.

In Norway, hooks at least five thousand years old have been found. These were fashioned from pieces of bone and formed with crude barbs by Stone Age man. Another, of bronze, not only barbed but eyed, was found in a rich man's grave, and has been dated AD 150. In Colombia, South America, hooks came to light during mining operations on a river bed. Some of these were of soft gold with roughly formed eyes but two of them were of an alloy of gold and copper, proved by assay, which have been dated c. 500 BC. Bronze hooks, barbed but with the eye end flattened and notched to hold the whipping secure were found in an area successively occupied from 400 BC by Greeks, Macedonians and Romans when a tomb was hit by a shell during a First World War bombardment. These hooks were clasped in the hands of a man whose bones have been

dated 200 BC. This find was providential. The soldiers' rations were short
and British officers used the hooks to fish a nearby lake full of carp, of
which they caught thousands, making a welcome addition to the diet of
the troops.

Parts of the Hook
Hook types and patterns are determined by the varying aspects of shank
length, shape, type of eye, the gape from point to shank, spear, barb, and
the type of point itself. See fig. 8.

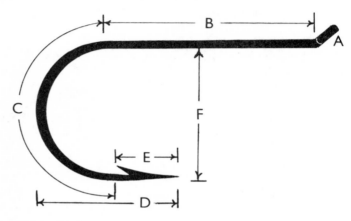

8   *Parts of the hook:*
              A   *Eye*   D   *Spear*
              B   *Shank*   E   *Barb and Point*
              C   *Shape*   F   *Gape*

Wire   Hooks are formed from wire used either in its normal state, when
it is termed 'regular' or to some extent flattened by forging, when it is
termed 'forged' or 'forged flat' (fig. 9).

REGULAR   FORGED

9   *Shank cross sections*
Forged are considered advantageous by some anglers since greater
strength is given to the shape which offers better resistance against
straightening by the fish. Diameter of wire is defined as 'fine,' 'standard'
or 'stout.' 'Fine' or 'standard' is better for dry flies than 'stout' since less
weight of wire is involved.

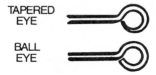

10   *Eyes*

Eyes   Eyes on trout hooks are mainly 'tapered' or 'ball' type (fig. 10). 'Tapered' is the most common but 'ball' eye are usually cheaper. Eyes are:

    TDTE (or TDE) being 'turned down tapered eye.'
    TUTE (or TUE) being 'turned up tapered eye.'
    TDBE   being 'turned down ball eye.'
    TUBE   being 'turned up ball eye.'

Ring eyes which are neither up nor down but level are occasionally referred to in fly patterns but are not in common use.

Shanks   Shanks are made in various lengths depending on the type of hook but in general terms 'X' is the definition of shank length. The thickness of wire, the gape, etc., is unchanged despite lengthening of the shank. To give examples, assume that hook sizes progress 1, 2, 3, 4, 5, 6. A size 3 hook with a 2X shank will have the standard shank length of a size 5 hook, i.e., the shank length of a hook two sizes larger, whilst a size 2 hook with a 4X shank will have the standard shank length of a size 6 hook, i.e., the shank length of a hook four sizes larger.

Long shank hooks are rarely used for wet and dry flies except for Mayfly patterns. These are made from fine wire and are 2X long in the shank, obtainable in up or down eye.

Spears   Hook spears are manufactured to run parallel with the shank or offset to one side or the other. Fig. 11 shows the shank flat on a surface and the spear rising from it to an exaggerated degree for clarity.

KIRBED   STRAIGHT   REVERSED

11   *Spears*

There are various views held as to why one type is preferable to another. Some feel the straight spear will be pulled out of the mouth of the fish because it is flat, their choice then being either kirbed or reversed since, although the fly may be lying sideways, the point protrudes and will penetrate immediately the angler applies pressure. The counter view appears to be that with a kirbed or reversed spear (a) the pull of the line puts an excessive amount of pressure against the side of the spear instead of concentrating it on the point for penetration, and (b) the fish will quickly feel the point of a kirbed or reversed spear and reject it before the angler can drive it home.

Barb   My experience has been the cheaper the hook the more rank the barb which may then prevent adequate penetration of the spear. The products of well-established hook makers are designed by experts and the barbs cut in the wire are adequate and neither too rank nor too shallow. In the 1920s there was quite a call for barbless hooks, presumably answering a call by the more kindly and considerate angler although it has been said that the demand arose from the wish of some purists to add a further handicap to success. These hooks were used more in the south of England than elsewhere. Instead of a barb being raised from the wire, the wire itself was bent to provide a small hump which acted in a similar way to a barb *but this form of barbless hook did not tear the fish* when removed and thus undersized fish could, it was claimed, be returned unharmed. This design, shown in fig. 12, was the invention of Mr W. J. Jamison of Chicago, USA.

12   Barbless hook of the 1920s

In recent years the reintroduction of barbless hooks, not necessarily to the above design, has again been advocated, sometimes by people who frown on angling as a sport and sometimes by anglers themselves. Bearing in mind the pain one feels when a hook is accidentally driven into some part of one's anatomy and making the assumption, rightly or wrongly, that fish feel pain, perhaps we ought to give the fish the benefit of the doubt and use barbless hooks. Do we really need to be persuaded?

Point   A great deal has been written of the advantage of one type of point over another but I take leave to doubt whether the average angler gives the question much consideration. This may arise from the purchase of flies from the local tackle shop where the decision as to the type of hook has been made by someone else. Those who tie their own flies can make their own choice disregarding previous practices and prejudices if they feel so inclined. In my view experiment is an enjoyable exercise. Fancy ideas may not prove effective when put to the test, but you are your own man, finding out for yourself. One only has to think of the past to realise that if others had not worked out and proved their own theories, so much of what we now accept as standard would never have come into being.

13 *Hollow*   *Spear*   *Curved in*

Gape The distance between the shank and the point is termed the gape. In some patterns the distance is increased and such hooks are then defined as 'wide gape,' a type popular for both wet and dry flies.

Size Scale Confusion is sometimes brought about by references in earlier angling literature to Redditch or New Scale. Long ago the hook makers of Redditch established a scale of sizing known as either Redditch or Old Scale but since this scale was born in the fish hook industry it bore some relation to the gauge of the wire used. The so-called Pennell (or New Scale) introduced by Cholmondely Pennell was known to few but those fishing dry fly, clearly a minority. So widespread was the confusion at one time that it was necessary to memorise or carry details of the conversion from one scale to another. Another scale, the Kendal, had been in existence earlier and, though falling into disuse, it made confusion worse confounded. Add to these the Model Perfect scale and it is not to be wondered at that other scales to end all scales have been suggested but, so far, Redditch prevails, although some amendment even to this is currently being advocated.

Since it may be of interest, a list of comparative trout hook sizes under the four scales is provided below, but it is the Redditch (or Old Scale) which is in use today, mainly limited to even number sizes.

Redditch (or Old Scale)	6	7	8	9	10	11	12	13	14	15	16	17	18
Pennell (or New Scale)	9	8	7	6	5	4	3	2	1	0	00	000	0000
Kendal Scale	8	7	6	5	4	3	2	1	0	00	000	—	—
Model Perfect scale	4	5	7	8	10	13	14	15	16	18	19	20	21

Trout hooks produced today are mainly bronzed but occasionally a silvered hook finds favour. The finish offers some protection against rust.

For trout fly-tying there are basically three styles currently popular:
Round bend – a good type for wet flies and for the smaller dry flies.
Limerick – usually of stouter wire and in consequence popular for wet
    flies needing a little more weight.
Sproat – for wet and dry flies.

14 Round bend   Limerick   Sproat

Need I say that cheap hooks never pay for they may be the cause of one losing the fish of a lifetime.

Threads, Tinsels, Wires, Wax and Varnish

There are those who adhere almost exclusively to silk and, in the opposite camp, those who prefer nylon. I feel that both have their uses at different times and for different purposes. Disabuse yourself of the thought that the 'silks' your wife has in her sewing box, even assuming you could plunder them with impunity, will suffice. They will not, except for larger patterns because, generally, they are too thick.

For small dry flies like midges a very fine thread is needed otherwise the body and head of the fly becomes too bulky for the pattern. Thread sizes run to a scale by diameter. 'A' is thickest and descending in diameter we have 2/0, 3/0, 4/0, 5/0, down to 18/0, this last for midges. In the smaller diameters there is usually a restriction in colours available.

Silk does not stretch, nylon does to some small degree. Both weaken in sunlight, silk particularly. Never buy silk taken from a shop window. When buying, remember that the spool on which it is provided has to fit your bobbin holder. Silks are available in many colours and Pearsall's, the most well-known supplier, lists the following:

'Gossamer' Tying Silks (fine), 45 m. reels – all colours as listed below.
'Naples' Tying Silks (medium), 45 m. reels – colours as listed below, with some exceptions (marked*).
'Marabou' Floss Silk (fine), 8 m. reels – colours as listed below, with some exceptions. (marked†).

No.	Colour	No.	Colour	No.	Colour
1	White	7*	Blue	13†*	Crimson
2†*	Straw	8	Purple	14	Claret
3†*	Primrose	9	Black	15†*	Maroon
4†	Light yellow	9a†*	Grey	16	Olive
5	Yellow	10†*	Ash	17	Brown
6†*	Amber	11†	Golden olive	18	Green
6a*	Light orange	11a	Scarlet	19	Hot orange
6b†*	Sherry spinner	12*	Cardinal	20*	Light olive

'Gossamer' is the usual fine silk used for fly-tying. 'Naples' is a medium silk but ideal for larger flies and lures. 'Marabou' is floss silk used for winding bodies. In nylon, fine thread 6/0 to 9/0 is about right for smaller wet and dry flies, 4/0 to 6/0 for larger wet flies.

Monocord is a flat, single filament thread which is particularly strong. It is ideal for ribbing bodies and will form neat tapered heads. Being 3/0 in size it is unsuitable for small flies.

Many silk and nylon threads are supplied unwaxed but there is a growing market for prewaxed thread and most suppliers stock both.

Body Floss
Many fly bodies are made simply by winding on floss which can be silk such as 'Marabou,' which is of twisted strands needing to be untwisted before use, or rayon which is flat. Both are supplied in a variety of colours. There is also acetate floss usable in the same way or, if a thinner such as nail varnish remover is applied to an acetate body, the floss becomes a malleable plastic and can be formed into flat or tapered shapes.

Fluorescent floss, the inclusion of which it is argued, improves the likelihood of the fish being attracted to the fly, can be used to form a small tip, wound on to form the body proper, used as a ribbing over other material or wound on as a head to the fly. Pastel shades only are usually provided.

Wool
Both natural and man-made, it is used to form fly bodies or, if fluorescent, as tips to other bodies.

Body Dubbings
Dubbing is the term used to describe material such as rabbit, seal or hare fur and man-made fibres in fine strands which can be spun round a base of silk or nylon thread, i.e., dubbed, and then wound on to form fly bodies. Polypropylene, nylon and other synthetics in a wide variety of colours are also used.

Latex
In sheet form this will produce a semi-translucent body when wound on and if a ribbing of black is laid over a white body and the latex then wound over both, the simulated fish skeleton can be seen through it to some extent. Liquid latex is also supplied which can be painted directly over a prepared body or on to a sheet of glass where it will dry to an almost transparent state and can then be used as in the sheet form.

Tinsels

These are supplied in silver and gilt and in three styles – flat, embossed and oval. Flat is used to provide a ribbing to a body of other material or to form the body proper. Embossed has a criss-cross or zig-zag pattern of lines or dots impressed upon it and is used mainly as a ribbing but occasionally for a proportion of the body. Oval is precisely that and made by winding a fine tinsel over a core of silk and is most preferred for ribbing bodies.

Round thread, probably due to its rather high cost, is less used today as a ribbing or for tags than in earlier times but is obtainable in both silver and gilt. Solid wire in fine diameters, silver and gilt, for ribbing bodies is an alternative to flat or oval. Tinsels and wires are occasionally supplied on cards but usually come on spools and it is one of life's small irritations that no-one has yet thought of some way other than the slit in the spool edge to affix the tinsel end to prevent the whole exploding into loose coils. Elastic bands will suffice but are not the ultimate solution.

Sizes are by numbers, the higher the number the smaller the diameter. A rough guide is:

Hook Size	16	14	12	10	8
Flat tinsel for body	1 or 2	1 or 2	1, 2 or 3	2 or 3	3 or 4
Flat tinsel for ribbing	1	1	2	2 or 3	3 or 4
Oval tinsel for ribbing	—	—	14	14	15
Wire for ribbing	27	27	26	26 or 25	25

Treat embossed as for flat in sizing.

Silver tinsels unless treated with a protective coating are liable to tarnish just sitting in the fly-tying box but the untreated type, if tarnished, can be brought back to former glory by a brisk rub with a piece of chamois leather.

Lead

Occasionally needed for weighting bodies, lead is available as wire in various thicknesses to suit the size of the fly. In times of adversity one may resort to the sheet lead with which some wine bottles are capped. This can be cut into thin strips and wound on as is the wire or laid over the upper part of the shank and bound on if one wishes the fly to turn over and travel point up, thus avoiding to some extent being caught in weed, etc., on the river bottom.

Copper wire is also used as an underbody to weight flies and is available in various thicknesses. The very fine is a little fragile but avoids bulk. In all wires and tinsels remember that kinks should be avoided for they cause irritating breaks at the worst moment. Synthetic tinsels which are light in weight and can be stretched to some degree when being wound on, are cheap and do not tarnish. They are sold on spools as strip in several widths and as thread in a form similar to oval tinsel. Other types are meshed tubing and plain sheet. The most well known names are Lurex or Mylar, seen mainly in gold and silver but occasionally in other colours.

Raffia
Both natural and plastic. The latter comes in a variety of colours, can form bodies and wing cases. Plastic raffia should be tied in and then wetted before being stretched to perform the necessary function for it will tighten up as it dries. If this is not done, when the raffia enters the water it will slacken and may lose its tidy form. Plastic string, if opened out, can also usefully perform the same functions.

Cork
Available in various forms such as sheet and squared or rounded lengths has its uses. In earlier days thin sheet cork made the body for the Mayfly and today small slips can be incorporated into a dressing to aid the floating capability of the fly. Bass bug bodies are also formed, obtained either ready made or shaped up by the tyer.

Wax
The most common is prepared fly-tying wax for application to the tying thread. Brown cobbler's wax and white beeswax can be used instead. Some soft or tacky wax is offered in handy polythene or hard plastic pots which some tyers prefer, particularly when applying dubbing, for which purpose liquid wax is also used. Since the latter contains a drying agent, the cap should always be replaced on the bottle, or the wax will thicken. In any case an uncapped bottle is likely to be knocked over as you will undoubtedly learn.

Varnish
The most common is celluloid varnish somewhat similar to nail varnish. Fly heads are secured with it and if hook shanks are painted with it immediately before body materials such as peacock or swan herls are wound on, this will make for more secure bodies which are unlikely to unwind if torn by the teeth of trout. You will find it has many other uses. Varnish may be had in clear, white, black, red, yellow, blue and green. A thinner is also sold with which to top up when the varnish thickens as the result of evaporation.

Some tyers prefer a brown spirit varnish for finishing fly heads but, whatever your choice, it is wise to use some form of stand in which there are depressions wherein the bottles are secure against accidents. Neither varnish nor wax is easy to remove from clothing or carpets.

Materials

A wealth of material is available to the fly-tyer. If one has but limited interest, it is advisable to select only the plumage, fur and hair necessary for the patterns ordinarily to be used. That is not to say there is not a great deal of pleasure to be derived from the search and acquisition of new materials but there is a tendency for these to accumulate and unless adequately packeted and clearly marked there is a danger that precious time can be spent in searching through a mass of what was once very attractive but is now just an untidy mess. The time can be used to better advantage in tying flies.

All fur and feather will attract insects which can mean ruin, particularly to choice capes. Press-close polythene bags have served me well for storage; they pack flat, are transparent and cheap and can be labelled with modern adhesive labels obtainable in all colours and sizes.

Plumage
Peacock Herl   Available as 'eyes,' on the quill or loose in packets, the latter often of poorer quality with meagre flue. It is used in a multitude of flies, mainly to form a bronze/green body (see *Coachman*). Off the main quill lead sub-quills and these, stripped of flue (the minute plumage attached to them) with an ordinary indiarubber, then provide bare quills which can be wound on to form the fly body. Those near to but not in the eye frequently have light and dark edges and this shows up as a form of segmentation (see *Blue Upright*). These sub-quills can also be bleached and then dyed various colours.
Peacock Sword   Irridescent brilliant green plumage used occasionally for bodies but more often for wings as in Alexandra.
Ostrich Herl   Available on the quill and packeted, usually of good quality either way. Somewhat longer in the flue than peacock and used for winding bodies of shrimps and sedges; in one sedge pattern the flue is barbered off to allow the quill to show through. Takes dye easily and is available in white and dyed all colours. Black can be wound through a white or cream hackle to give a black centre simulating a badger hackle – black centre with white edges.
Turkey   The tail feathers of these birds provide an ideal fly body simply by winding a small number of fibres round the hook shank. These fibres have a fine flue and thus are excellent for slim-bodied patterns. Such tails come in various natural colours – cinnamon, oak (simulating the marking of this wood), very dark brown and almost black. Cinnamon for sedge bodies, oak for Muddler wings and the almost black for such patterns as Lunn's Caperer. Turkey fibres also make up good wing cases for nymphs.
Turkey Marabou   A fluffy feather not used in any of the patterns set out herein but much used for the wings of lures – Appetiser is one. Available

in white and dyed all colours, it is rather fragile.

Swan   A slightly more substantial fibre than turkey is obtained from the wings of this bird, having the same uses and supplied in many dyed colours. Rather thick where the fibres join the quill but of sufficient length to avoid using that part when tying medium-to-small flies.

Goose   Shoulder feathers have a fine fibre and flue. In natural white or dyed colours they are ideal for fly bodies. Primary feathers are also used for the same purpose. Canada geese provide a pale grey/buff feather whilst barnacle geese somewhat darker grey/brown quills. All can be dyed.

Cock Pheasant   The central tail feather is used in many dressings. Two or three fibres form the tails for Mayflies whilst several wound on together will form the body, and the butt ends, tied back over the hook shank, will form the wings, as in Simple Fredsedge. Sawyer's Nymph, a very successful fly, utilises these fibres in conjunction with copper wire. When selecting these feathers seek those which, when viewed from the underside, are as mahogany coloured as possible. The longer the fibre the better – they are the type most needed. Wing cases for nymphs can also be formed with fibres from it. Other feathers from the bird are occasionally useful.

Hen Pheasant   The primary and secondary wing feathers provide slips with which to make up the wings on patterns such as the March Brown, whilst the central tail feather is used for the same purpose in others, Invicta for example.

Mallard   Wing feathers from the drake have many uses; the white satin underfeathers for the wings of Coachman, the blue portion of the white-tipped outer feathers for Butcher and, with a portion of the white tip included, for the Heckham Peckham. The grey quills also make up into nice wings although compared with coot, for instance, they have more substance and are a little more opaque, which is not desirable in some patterns. Breast feathers, of light and dark grey stippled appearance, formed the wings of the once popular Fan Wing Mayfly. On mature birds the flank feathers tend to bronze and are much sought after for Mallard and Claret and other patterns needing a dark stippled wing. Since there are but a few to a bird they are rather expensive. Smaller grey stippled flank feathers, dyed a fawn colour, are good substitutes for summer duck used to hackle Straddlebug Mayfly. Altogether the drake is a very useful bird providing both food and feather but of the duck only a few feathers are used, principally those of the neck, shoulder and flank.

Golden Pheasant   This very decorative bird supplies us with crest feathers (otherwise known as toppings) from the crown of the bird. These are the golden stranded feathers much used as overlay for salmon fly wings and in the smaller sizes for tails of trout flies, as in Rogan's Olive. Below the crown the bird has a collar of tippet feathers, hot orange in colour with black tips and a black bar. Several fibres will make the tail for Mallard and Claret, the Teal series and other sea-trout flies. Body feathers of orange/ red, neck feathers of fan shape and green with a sheen, are used for some more exotic patterns.

Teal and Widgeon   Breast and flank feathers, of clear black and white stippling, form the wings of Peter Ross, Blue Charm and sea-trout flies. Wing feathers are used for Wickham.

Partridge   Brown back feathers for hackles, for example March Brown, speckled tail feathers for wings of sedges and brown tail feathers for Grannom and others. Brown body feathers are also used for the sparse hackles of spiders. Grey breast feathers provide the hackle for the light version of Partridge and Orange and other spider-like flies.

Grouse   Brown mottled wing feathers make up the wings on all the Grouse series of flies, Grouse and Green for example.

Coot   Wing feathers are used to make up wings for dry flies as an alternative to our home-bred blackbird and starling. They are a little darker, hence admirable for Blue Winged Olive.

Starling   The wing feather is now most commonly used for wet flies such as Greenwell and dry flies such as Large Dark Olive. It can also be obtained dyed blue for the wings of Iron Blue. Breast feathers provide the hackles for many patterns, including Black Gnat and needle flies. These breast feathers have a white tip and the addition of a touch of golden yellow enamel over a small eye of typist's *Snopake* or *Liquid Paper* makes an acceptable substitute for the very scarce junglecock now banned for export from India. The starling body skin and wings are very oily and need to be kept separately from other materials and in polythene bags.

Moorhen   Certain of the underwing feathers are useful for wet, hackled patterns such as Waterhen Bloa.

Woodcock   The wing feathers of dark brown have a light brown zig-zag pattern on the outer edge and these provide the patterned wings for the flies in the Woodcock series of wet flies (see *Woodcock and Green*).

Snipe   Adherence to the correct pattern for Snipe and Purple (which see) demands the use of a small underwing feather which is very dark, almost black, for the hackle. The snipe primary wing feathers provide the wing slips for Blue Dun and Dark Bloa.

Jay   The blue-barred feathers on the leading edge of the wing provide the front hackle originally specified for Invicta. Alas, many fly-tyers found their preparation for this purpose rather troublesome and if these fibres are now used at all as the beard hackle for Invicta, they are frequently torn or cut from the quill and tied in as a bunch. Shop-bought patterns frequently have blue dyed guinea fowl (Gallena) fibres incorporated instead of jay. Blue jay will also brighten any feathered decoration you might care to wear in your hat, as I do!

Heron   Fibres, blue/grey in colour from hackles, six to eight inches long, of the bird affectionately called 'Old Nog' or from his wing feathers make nice fly bodies when wound on the hook shank for Olives and as in Kite's Imperial. Frequently dyed a darker colour, my own preference is to steep them in picric acid to impart a beautiful olive tint. Care should be taken when using picric acid (see page 57).

Condor   This large South American bird has wings covering a very wide span from which herls are obtained up to four inches long bearing quite substantial flue, ideal material for fly bodies and widely used at the turn of the century. I hope that it was not to meet the demands of fly-tyers alone that these birds were decimated but this material is certainly very scarce now. Condor is normally replaced, although not adequately I feel, by swan.

All quills for winging, mallard for example, *should be kept in matched pairs,* i.e., a quill taken from the same position on each wing and paired up, since fly wings are made by taking a slip from each feather and tying them in together.

Fur and Hair

Fur and hair have long been known as useful fly-tying material. Charles Cotton mentioned 'spaniel's fur,' 'down of a fox-cub,' 'camel's hair,' 'dubbing of a white weasel's tail' in 1676. The American Indian is reputed long ago to have used fine strips of animal skin with the hair attached which he then bound in some way to a crude form of hook. Could it have been palmered? Not having seen one I cannot tell. More recently in the 1930s Lee Wulff introduced his Wulff series of patterns (see *Grey Wulff*) incorporating fur bodies and hair wings.

Bucktail   Hair, 2 to 4 in. long, rather coarse, occasionally with a slight crinkle, in natural white and black and all shades of brown. White and light colours are frequently dyed. For wings, tips need to be aligned somewhat. The end cap of a ballpoint pen is useful but suppliers sell a tool made for this purpose.

Calftail   Crinkly hair, finer than bucktail and shorter, being 1 to 1½ in. long except at the tip which has longer hairs. Used for wings as in Little Dorrit and for wings on lure patterns, Whisky Fly for example. Dyed colours are wide ranging plus natural, white and almost black.

Grey Squirrel   Tail hair mostly called for in fly-tying. Occasionally as tails employing three or four fibres or chopped up to mingle with fur as a hairy dubbing. Greatest use is for wings of lures where the white tips take dye well. Tails are also bleached and dyed to provide an all-over colour. Body fur is also used as a dubbing.

Red Squirrel   Available only by import, the red/brown fur and tail hair is used in the same way as its grey cousin.

Mink   The escape of this animal from fur farms has resulted in the rapid growth of small colonies, particularly in south-west England where it is trapped and shot as a pest because it preys on game birds and other animals. The mink has fine silky fur, hence its attraction for the fair sex, and is an excellent dubbing material for fly bodies. It comes in light and dark brown, white and natural blue dun. The longer guard hairs are useful for dry fly tails whilst the tail underfur is also good for dubbing.

Moose   The hollow, supple hair of the mane is obtainable in natural grey/brown and white. The latter takes dye and felt-pen colouring well if it is degreased beforehand. The fine tips provide tails and the remainder winds on to show a slightly tapering body. That of the Orange Quill is a good example. One white and one, sometimes two, grey/brown hairs wound on together as a body simulate well the segmented bodies of natural flies.

Red Fox   Reynard's long guard hairs make winging material and the springy underfur dubbing for bodies.

Grey Fox (imported)   The guard hairs on this animal are barred black and white. Anyone wishing to experiment with hair wings for dry flies might find these attractive since they can be dyed but retain the barred effect. Underfur of the grey fox is grey/brown, again used as dubbing.

Hare   Fur of the English hare has been included in fly dressings for at least two hundred years. There is a multitude of such dressings, notably the Gold Ribbed Hare's Ear for which short ear hair or body fur can be utilised for the fly body except near the eye of the hook where longer hairs from the edge of the ear are incorporated. These same ear hairs form the tail. More often, all the material for this fly is taken from the various parts of the hare's ear. Body fur makes excellent dubbed bodies whilst the whiskers can be dyed and wound on to create a fly body or used to rib a body of other material. Whisker tips also make fine tails. Ears alone or whole mask are freely obtainable.

Wild Rabbit   The common grey rabbit has blue/grey underfur, the tips of the fur being brown. Underfur is much used (see *Grey Duster*) since it is soft and one of the easiest to use as dubbing. Various parts of the body provide different shades of light and dark fur whilst the undertail gaves white.

Domestic Rabbit   One such animal is a beautiful blue dun colour and running a fine comb through its fur will provide a superb dubbing. On black rabbits the underfur is not black but often a grey/blue, another excellent dubbing, as is the fur from white rabbits. All such fur is very soft and silky and easy to use. All lighter colours take dye well.

Mole   This little animal has very short fur of dark grey which can be used as it comes or subjected to the dye bath to impose a tint. My own preference is to steep the skin in picric acid which imparts a most satisfactory olive tint. Skins are approximately 5 by 3½ in. and the fur is usually pinched from the skin for use as dubbing. Being short fur there is the advantage that the colour of the silk used will itself tint the appearance of the fur to some extent, provided it is dubbed on thinly.

Muskrat   Widely used in the United States but somewhat less so in the United Kingdom, the muskrat fur is ideal dubbing material being darkish blue/grey on the back and somewhat lighter blue/grey on the underparts of the animal.

Domestic Dog   I well remember reading 20 odd years ago about a fly called Dogsbody to provide the material for which the tyer had combed his pet dog. From that day onward I have developed the habit of sizing up pet dogs with fly-tying in mind. A good combing of a thick-furred dog such as the Chow-chow produces a wealth of dubbing material mostly fine and silky. Somewhere else I read of a man combing a black greyhound which gave him blue dun dubbing. I have spoken to many owners and they have never objected to my combing their dogs, rather the reverse, showing pride when told the purpose. One word of warning – be sure the dog is as amenable as the owner!

Deer   Body hair is hollow and thus an aid to the floating properties of the fly. One particular use for it was introduced by Don Gapen in his Muddler Minnow, the ball-shaped head of which is made by flaring a number of deer body hairs round the hook shank by applying two *loose* turns when tying in. Pulling the silk will then get them to flare when they will look somewhat akin to a wound hackle. Many additions of hair are needed which are then trimmed to shape. The same process can be used to create the body on sedge patterns where the majority of the shank is so covered and clipped to shape.

Woodchuck (*common groundhog*)   From the body fur the guard hairs have a use for winging many types of fly, whilst the underfur, almost black, makes a good dubbing. The tail hair, dark brown in colour, makes ideal winging material particularly as the hairs are even in length and therefore less fussy to handle.

Oppossum (*Australian*)   This fur is very soft with good blending properties. It makes excellent dubbing, the natural colours ranging over black, through grey/blue to white and pale yellowish cream to tan.

Seal   This is a fur with a glint to it rarely seen in any other fur. Thus the thorax of a fly made up with seal fur has little sparkles of light when examined in a good light. As a test of this I suggest you compare the body of a fly tied with sheep's wool against another tyed with seal fur. I think you will find that the seal fur is more translucent and odd fibres protruding will have a sparkle absent from wool. Some seal fur from suppliers is much too coarse – fine fur is needed. The natural colour of the pup's fur is a creamy white but it is obtainable dyed in many colours since it is a popular and much used material.

Other fur and hair is used in fly-tying where almost anything will be found useful by someone. Have you ever looked at your wife's fur coat? Or her fur wrap, or hat, or . . .? Furriers sometimes have snippets and cuttings which they may be willing to part with. Such fur will usually be soft and silky and beautifully dyed.

For dubbing, fur and/or underfur is also used from the beaver, otter (coarse), racoon, water animals, guinea pigs and combings of the domestic cat, but watch for unwanted guests in the latter!

Capes (or Rooster Necks)

The name cape is given to that portion of the skin and feathers from the crown to the base of the back of the neck of the domestic fowl which provides the hackles we use to simulate the legs and tails of natural flies. These hackles are graded in size by nature, the smallest from the area at the crown and increasing in length and width as they descend to the base of the neck where the cape ends. A high quality cape may provide hackles to cover a wide range of hook sizes from 18, and even smaller, to 10. With a poorer quality cape the range of flies it will cater for becomes more limited because there are usually fewer small hackles.

Remember the *larger* the hook number the *smaller* the hackle needed for it. Thus a size 12 hook with a hackle from the very crown of the bird would look like 'A' in fig. 15, whilst a size 20 hook tied with a hackle from the vase of the neck would appear as in 'B.' Both are out of proportion for the intended purpose which is, in the main, to simulate the legs of the fly represented by the pattern.

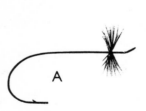
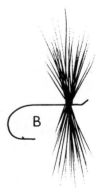

15   *Matching hackle to hook*

Descriptions of the grades of capes may vary in different parts of the world and from one supplier to another who may show best grade as A, second quality as B, third quality as C and so on, or 1, 2, 3, 4, or Supergrade, Superior, Regular and Bargain. Whether all are graded on the same basis of selection I somehow doubt. Considering the price one can be called upon to pay for some types perhaps it is time a standard was introduced, if only for the guidance of the inexperienced. This is not to say that suppliers will provide one with a B when one orders an A – no such thing – but some gradings fall short of others, hence an A from one may be obtainable as a B from another, probably at lower cost.

Hackles can be obtained in small quantities in packets but are best on a cape which will provide hackles for dozens of flies.

Cock Bird

Good quality cock hackles should be springy, quickly recoiling to the natural position if bent over and released. They should have sparkle and a glossy sheen when examined in sunlight. The better the quality the narrower the hackle will be for its length, that is the individual fibres on the centre quill will be short up the whole length of the hackle.

Generally it is held that the best, glossiest, springy hackles for dry flies can be obtained only from mature birds of about three years, although I have heard other views. Certainly the cape should be taken when the bird is in prime condition.

Poor grade hackles, that is those which have much central web and are therefore unsuitable for dry flies, can be used for wet flies although there is still a certain amount of unwanted stiffness to the fibres when compared with a hackle from a hen cape.

Spade Hackles The name defines the shape of the tips of these hackles which will be found on the neck just outside the area of the normal cape and at the lower end. They will be found useful for tails generally and for beard hackles on wet flies.

Saddle Hackles These come from that part of the bird which, were it a horse, would hold the saddle, in the depression between the neck and the rump. Saddle hackles are very large, 3½ to 4½ in. in length, with glossy, springy, long fibres at the tip end. Ideal for tails and for wings of lures and salmon flies needing large, long-fibred hackles.

Tail Feathers Some cockerels have long, curled, dark, glossy, green-sheened tail feathers which I have found useful for wing cases, in beetles for example.

Hen Bird

Capes are cut from the hen bird in the same way as for the cock but there the similarity ends. Where the cock hackle is long and spearlike with springy, glistening fibres, the hen hackle is blunt ended, lacks lustre and is made up of soft, heavily webbed fibres.

16   Normal hen hackle

Since these fibres readily soak up water they are excellent for wet fly patterns where the play of the current will give them life and movement.
Saddle Hackles   These are not long as in the cock saddle hackle, but simply larger than the normal hen hackles. These larger saddle hackles are ideal for the wings of dry flies such as those in the Clarke/Goddard USD dun patterns. These are cut with a wing cutter to provide the wing shape attached to the quill ready for tying-in.
Pin Feathers   These are the immature feathers. Capes containing too great a number should be avoided for not only are the feathers unusable but it generally denotes either that the bird was not fully mature or was not in prime condition when it was killed.

Hackle Colours
There are many specific recognised 'colours' in hackles, as the following illustrates.
White or without colour. Pure white is a rarity greatly valued and most of us have to accept 'not quite white' which, nevertheless, in good quality is not all that common but useful for dyeing. A cock cape having good quality *small* hackles is always worth acquiring. Cream can be of varying density, some very pale, some with more of a deep cow-cream appearance. In my experience the deeper the cream the better the hackle for dry flies where a cock cape is concerned.
Honey, a very rich golden, creamy colour between cream and light ginger.
Honey Dun, as honey above, but with a centre web of light mousy grey. Rare in high quality – see it, buy it and hang the expense!
Ginger in the lighter specimens will be a rich straw colour and the addition of a hint of red will give pale ginger. More red and a little buff deepens the ginger to what would be considered usual for the name, still fairly light in overall colour. Dark ginger comes with the addition of still a little more red with a touch of brown.
Light Red Game virtually commences where dark Ginger ends. More solid colour, a sort of Reynard red/brown with a hint of gold. Very popular.
Medium Red Game descends a little deeper in the shade – one of the most used hackles. Also known as Red Island Red.
Dark Red Game tends to a greater degree of brown with an appearance of inbuilt fire to the individual fibres.
Chocolate is a rich, warm colour rarely specified in dressings but of the

sort one would feel would be an inspiration to the tyer. Not all that commonly seen.

Furnace, as the name indicates, has a real touch of fire to it with a black web up the centre. A rich, warm, glowing, light mahogany describes it. A high-quality dry fly cape is a treasure.

Coch-y-bondhu is very similar to furnace but the tip of each fibre is black as is the centre web. A really good specimen will be prized. There is a very dark, fiery red type also to be had and when seen should be snapped up – you will not regret the purchase.

Andalucian Blue, one of the most prized of capes, less used now than formerly, no doubt due to its rarity and hence cost. I have one before me as I write, given to me by a bird fancier, bless her. It is a very, very dark fire red with a dark, almost black web, to which there is a beautiful blue/green sheen. On the back of the hackle the red outer edges are a lighter furnace red whilst the web appears black with an exceptional blue sheen.

Brown is precisely that and without any touch of fire to it. Mostly darkish but to make up for the lack of warm glow some have an exceedingly good gloss and the individual hackles sparkle in good light.

Badger, a very popular hackle with a black, or at least almost black, centre web and off-white through palest cream to real cream outside the web. A pure white with a really black web is scarce and even more so in first-class dry fly quality. In a few such capes there is an icy, silvery white. The capes are then called Silver Badger, very rare indeed. I once picked up reasonably cheaply a superb white on jet black badger cape with a difference: the tips were also black. Alas, someone else had a desire for it and it disappeared during one of my fly-tying classes. I had not tied a single fly from it and have not had the good fortune to find another cape like it since. There's a moral in that somewhere.

Golden Badger, as the name indicates, has a warm golden-yellow appearance which I find attractive. I have tied some very nice Grey Duster variants, for want of a better name, using these hackles, which do very well when the sun is low on the horizon. I can only surmise that the reason is that the hackle picks up and accentuates the fiery red glow of the sun and this motivates the fish to take. Is this pure conjecture on my part or is there a supporting scientific reason?

Speckled Badger is the normal badger with a dark, nearly black speckle to the white or cream area which gives the fibres a nice broken look when wound on.

Light Blue Dun, sometimes called Pale Blue Dun. Dun is a light mousy grey and if one can imagine the addition of a light touch, of brown, blue and just a hint of purple-bronze, that would be about it. Difficult to find in good dry fly quality and we generally have to resort to dyed capes.

Medium Blue Dun, or just Blue Dun, is somewhat akin to the underfur of the common rabbit in colour and an unsullied cape of the one colour overall in the natural state would be a rare beauty if of high dry fly quality. Most are dyed, which can produce some odd but useful quirks of colour.

Dark Blue Dun in a quality cape for dry fly is again a rarity. Sometimes called Iron Dun it really is dark heading almost into black. Dyed specimens are usually used instead.

Black in the natural is never quite jet black but is a black which seems slightly dusted with grey. Dyed capes are jet black, no doubt about that.

Cree is a cape with cross bands of two colours darker than the main cape colour. Were the cape mainly pale ginger the bands might be of dark red game and almost black. Some, in addition to the banding, have a fleck of lighter spotting on the darker areas. Many shades.

Fleck comes in all shades from light to darkish background with a fleck or dapple of a different colour. Quite a considerable number of variations can be found which can produce some interesting effects if one is an experimenter.

Grizzle is the description given to a cape the hackles on which are basically white with a very slight bluish tinge, barred horizontally with black. The black bars have a green sheen to them. A very good price will be demanded for a dry fly cape of quality.

Variants. Inevitably there occurs mixing of breeds, and capes from the resulting progeny should be shunned, or actively sought, depending on one's attraction to such multi-coloured, flecked, speckled, badgered and 'Heinz' specimens which quite often are of surprisingly good quality and reasonably priced.

Origin

Due to broiler production methods the number of free-ranging domestic fowls has declined in recent years. Broiler chickens do not, unfortunately, reach maturity and in consequence the hackles are usually of very poor, soft quality. As a result, prime capes are mainly imported from China or India, the latter usually providing capes of a smaller size.

The increase in the numbers of fly-tyers has brought into being establishments which specialise in producing capes of high quality from specially bred birds with the fly-tyer in mind. Natural blue dun and grizzle in particular can be had but also other types. Such capes are costly but it is to be hoped that with such a large market in the offing the production of these fine quality capes will increase with a corresponding reduction in the price.

The method of obtaining capes through photo-dyeing as described by Eric Leiser in *Fly-Tying Materials* (1973) has not yet reached its full potential. The process involves the use of silver nitrate, an expensive ingredient, photographic developer then an acetic acid solution as a neutraliser. Finally, the dyeing, if that is the right description, has to be fixed or set by photographic hypo. A wide range of duns is possible, including bronze. The process improves the sheen to the hackles which really sparkle and some commercial enterprises already market them. I anticipate that the practice will spread.

Picric Acid

Materials can be steeped in a saturated solution of picric acid to impart a superb yellowy-olive tint but care in using it is absolutely essential. There is no neeed for concern provided certain rules are adhered to, which are:

Metal   The solution *must not* be permitted to come into contact with metal in any way.

Source   The solution can be obtained from a dispensing chemist and is referred to as a 'saturated solution of picric acid.' You will be asked to explain the purpose for which it is required after which, assuming your explanation is accepted, it will be sold to you in a small-necked *glass* container.

Processing Dish   A glass, plastic or glazed earthenware vessel of some sort *must* be used, *never metal* of any kind either to contain the solution or to remove materials from it. I use a shallow ovenware glass casserole dish.

Processing   Pour the solution into the dish in sufficient quantity to cover all you intend to tint. A couple of really small glass bottles filled with water and capped (plastic caps only) make ideal weights to keep the materials beneath the surface. Alternatively, a wide-necked *glass* bottle can be used for the longer items such as swan or goose quills as they can be pressed vertically into the liquid, but hackles need to be tied in bunches with thin string or cotton to enable them to be extracted easily.

Materials to be Treated   Dun or light-coloured hackles tied into small bunches by the butts, ostrich herl, grey heron, swan, goose (white and buff), and other wing feathers, seal fur, coiled-up nylon leaders, natural and artificial fur and similar materials can all be treated by immersion. Two hours is sufficient to tint, longer for a more dense treatment. It will be necessary to wash materials such as wing primaries in detergent of some kind to remove any natural grease, but usually the less they are handled the better.

Safe Handling   If you have cuts or abrasions on your hands wear rubber gloves when using the process. It is, of course, elementary that the solution should be kept away from the mouth and eyes, out of the reach of children and animals, and your glass dish out of the kitchen.

Extracting Materials   Remembering the rule that no metal must be used, a pair of plastic tongs, as used by photographers in the dark room, is ideal for the removal of materials from the dish and can be obtained from photographic shops. The tinted materials should then be rinsed in a *plastic* bucket of water and laid out on a sheet of newspaper or something similar. In a warm atmosphere they will soon dry out.

Disposal of Solution   Picric acid in solution loses some of its strength in time. If you decide to dispose of it, pour it down the lavatory when the solution will be weakened by the flushing process and carried away safely without harm to the environment. *Do not* pour it down your metal sink, nor into drains with metal grids. The roots of your hydrangeas or other shrubs won't like it either.

Used sensibly, bearing the foregoing points in mind, picric acid treatment of materials can be most helpful in producing the yellowy-olive tints we find so attractive.

3

Ways and Means

Quality of Hackles
The hackle shown on the left in fig. 17 below is of good quality since it has little centre web, whilst that on the right has too much web and is, therefore, of poorer quality. On either side of the central quill every hackle has an area of web where the individual fibres have a fluffier appearance. The less web the better the hackle for dry flies since the web

17

is water absorbent, something we do not want. A dressing may name a particular type of hackle, for example medium red game, to be wound on behind the eye of the hook and, for the tail, fibres of the same type. The hackle to be wound on will be taken from a position approaching the crown end of the cape but the tail fibres from a larger hackle at the lower

end of the neck. Fibres for use as tails or for beard hackles on wet flies are best obtained from the hackle in the following manner.

Hold the tip 'A' of the hackle in the thumb and forefinger of the left hand and, with the other hand, pull the fibres downward so that the hackle then appears as in fig. 18. Gather the tips of the required number of fibres together into a bunch with the thumb and forefinger and tear them progressively from the centre quill in a downward movement towards the but end 'B.'

Doubling the Hackle for Wet Flies
When tying wet flies using wound hackles the fibres need to lean back from the eye thus:

19

This can be achieved quite simply by doubling one side of the hackle over to the other before the hackle is wound on. Tie in the butt end behind the eye of the hook. Clip a pair of hackle pliers on to the tip of the hackle and keep the hackle in tension whilst the left hand gathers the hackle fibres from the right side of the hackle and pulls them firmly across to the left. Work your way up and down the hackle until all but the extreme ends are pulled over to the left of the central quill. The hackle can then be wound on with all the points of the fibres leaning back from the eye of the hook.

Beard (or false) Hackles
On wet flies hackles are either wound on (see 'A' in fig. 20) so that fibres surround the body and lean back towards the tail, or a bunch of fibres is tied in to project from beneath the body a little back from the eye and towards the hook point ('B'). For the latter method, fibres are best torn from a large hackle since, when these are tied in, the excess protrudes well beyond the eye and can be gripped and lifted to facilitate a clean cut close to the hook shank. Where short fibres are used the excess is usually too

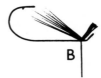

20

short to grip and time is wasted fiddling with the removal of the short
waste ends ('C') to ensure a neat result.

Dry Fly Hackles
One question I am constantly asked is how I manage to wind on a number
of turns of hackle in a narrow space without later turns forcing the earlier
wound fibres out of place. The answer is simply to draw the tips of the
fibres (of turns of hackle already wound) gently back towards the bend of
the hook whilst the next turn is taken. I stress 'gently' for the fibres must
not be flattened, merely moved out of the way of the succeeding turn.

Another little trick is to pull the fibres outward from the shank when
the fly is completed and the hackle tip secured. If the centre quill of the
hackle has been twisted a little when winding it on, the fibres on it will
tend to lean in the direction of the twist. Pulling the fibres and working
progressively round them all will assist, to a large degree, in straightening
the quill and thus the fibres will project at right angles to the shank. This
operation can improve the aesthetic appearance of the fly.

Dubbing
Dubbing is a very old term used to describe both the material, such as
mole or rabbit fur, and the method of wrapping it around the tying silk
which is then wound on to the hook shank to form the body of a fly. The
procedure is illustrated in fig. 21 and in the following notes.

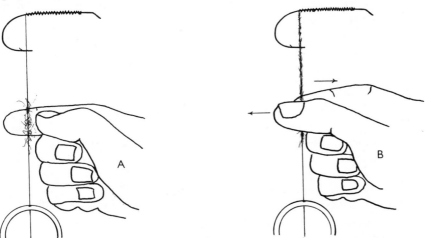

21

Assuming the hook is in the vice and the silk attached to it, well wax the
silk and then draw the bobbin of silk towards you. Pick up *a pinch* of dubbing material and with this on the ball of the forefinger, place it under and

against the silk (see 'A'). Compress the dubbing between thumb and fore-finger and roll it round the silk by moving the thumb to the left and the forefinger to the right (see 'B'). *Release* the thumb and forefinger and, without adding more dubbing, repeat the rolling so that the dubbing closely surrounds the silk. Slide the rolled dubbing up the silk to where it joins the hook and repeat the operation of adding more dubbing and rol-ling it on until there is sufficient to form the required body.

If the body is to be tapered do not thicken the amount of dubbing on the silk but simply wind on more turns of thinly dubbed silk to provide the taper. Do not apply too much dubbing to the silk or you will find that when the silk is wound round the hook shank the silk and the dubbing will have a tendency to separate. This is particularly so when using seal fur.

Stripped Hackle Quills
A number of patterns specify a stripped hackle quill to be wound on to form the body as in Lunn's Particular for example.

Because it is thinner at the tip end than at the butt, a stripped hackle will provide a slightly thickening body as it is wound towards the eye. For Lunn's Particular the hackle specified is Rhode Island Red, the centre quill of which is pale reddy-brown but, on the sides of the quill where the fibres are torn off, the quill is lighter and has tiny marks where the fibres originally joined it. Care is, therefore, needed in keeping the quill on the same plane when winding it on if the same colouring and marking is to obtain over the whole body. If the hackles are old or have been dyed they may well be a little brittle and it may pay to soak the quills in warm water to ensure they are pliable for winding on. Stripping the hackles merely involves removing the fibres from each side by pulling them downward towards the butt end.

Stripped Peacock Quills
Dry fly bodies in some patterns such as Blue Upright call for the use of stripped peacock quills. The easiest way to strip them is to lay them on a hard surface, press the middle finger on one end and the thumb on the other. Keep the quill stretched whilst an ordinary indiarubber is used to rub off the short flue. If the quills are to be dyed they can be stripped as above and then dyed. Alternatively, unstripped quills can be immersed in household bleach which will remove the flue and lighten the quill ready for dyeing. If the bleaching method is used the whole eye should be immersed but not for too long or the quills will seriously be weakened.

Teal Wings
The method adopted by nature to join up the individual fibres of feathers is to provide matching edges with a form of zip fastener (fig. 22).

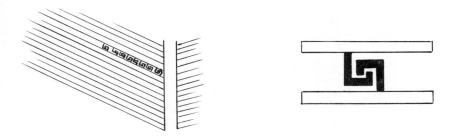

22 *Nature's sip fastener on a wing feather*

For the bird to obtain lift in the air, the 'zips' joining its wing fibres must be closed (or zipped up) otherwise the air flows through the openings and lift is reduced. No doubt the reader has seen a bird preening itself and one operation it performs is to run its beak through its wing feathers checking that all its zips are done up. The zips on the fibres of some birds are strong, on geese for instance, but on teal they are rather weak in the flank feathers and it is for this reason that wings of teal are not considered the easiest to tie in tidily and neatly.

The usual process is to cut a slip from a feather from the left side of the bird and a matching slip from a feather from the right side of the bird. These are then placed back to back, best sides outward and tied in together.

There is another method, however. Select a flank feather where the fibres on both sides of the central quill are of the same length (see 'A' of fig. 23). Cut away the centre quill and attached fibres so far down from the tip of the feather as is equal to the length of wing desired ('B'). Measure down the stem the width of the desired wing and tear off all the fibres (on both sides of the quill) below that point ('C'). Hold the butt of the central quill in one hand and stroke the wing fibres away with the other. Moistening the stroking fingers helps ('D'). The feather is then laid over the body of the fly so that the fine tips extend to the distance required. Use the first finger and thumb carefully to fold the two together. When satisfied with their positioning they can be tied in but the fingers holding the wings need to grip firmly and as near to the point of tying as possible.

Winging
The one essential ingredient to success is to keep the wing slips between the finger and thumb *tightly* compressed for, if you fail to do so, the wings will either split along the length of the fibres or they will lean out of the vertical and towards the line of pull applied by the silk. (See fig. 24.)

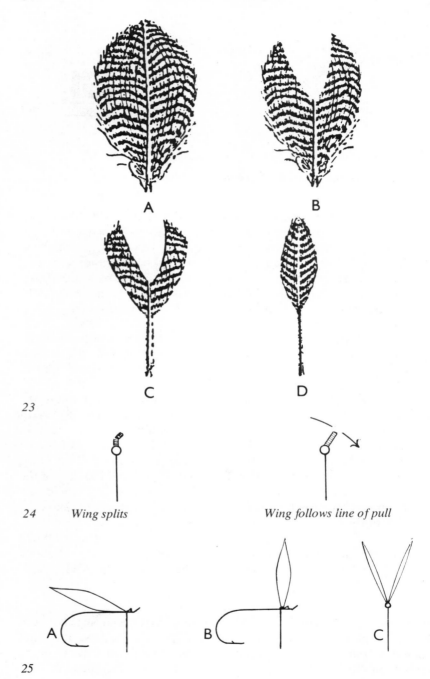

23

24   *Wing splits*   *Wing follows line of pull*

25

There are at least two ways of attaching wings for dry flies (fig. 25).

'A' shows the wings tied in wet fly style. In 'B' the wings are lifted to the vertical and one turn of silk taken round them at the point where they join the shank, followed by two turns round the shank only and tight up against the bend side of the wings to help to hold them erect. The wings in 'C' are then separated with a dubbing needle and a figure-of-eight tying applied.

Another way requires the wings to be incorporated initially in an advanced position as follows.

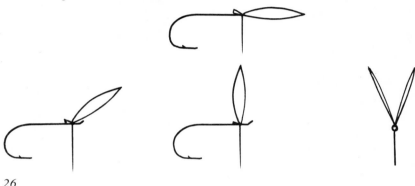

26

Thereafter there are two options. One is to lift the wings to an angle of 40° over the eye and secure them in that position. The other is to lift the wings to the vertical, secure, then separate with a dubbing needle and keep them separated with a figure-of-eight binding. Wings can be –

1. Paired slips cut from primary or secondary wing feathers, for instance, starling as in Orange Quill.

2. Bunches of fibres from a hackle or flank feather as in Light Cahill.

3. Bunches of hair as in Little Dorrit.

Many other materials have been tried in the past – pike scales, cuttings from tea bags, crinkly nylon fibres and, lately, polythene for spinner wings as in USD Poly-Red Spinner.

From an aesthetic point of view paired slips produce a pleasing finish to a fly but after a few casts or mouthing by a fish they are prone to split up into separated fibres hence there is a leaning towards bunches of hackle fibres or hair which are, in any case, less opaque than wings of solid fibre.

Figure-of-Eight

This is the form of security applied to dry fly wings to ensure that they remain in position and divided. Once the wings are tied in, the two slips (or the hackle fibres or hairs if these are used) have to be separated with a dubbing needle to form two separate wings.

Richard Walker gave this advice many years ago and it is as effective now as it was then (see also fig. 27):

Silk under (the hook shank) *straight* ('A' and 'C')
Silk over (the hook shank) *diagonally* ('B' and 'D')

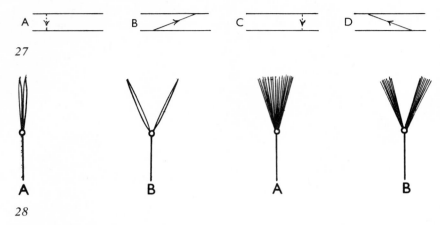

27

28

'A' (see fig. 28) is as first tied in and lifted to the vertical. 'B' is after separation and addition of figure-of-eight binding.

Secure Bodies

As a ribbing serves to protect a body so will varnish when applied to an underbody over which will be wound pheasant tail fibres or peacock/ostrich herl, for example. Coat the underbody, allow the varnish to become tacky and wind the material over it. This is a Richard Walker idea of many years standing.

Ribbing

When incorporating a ribbing be it silk, tinsel, lurex, stripped hackle quill or wire into a dubbed body such as of seal fur, there is a tendency for the ribbing to sink into the joints in the body winding if both the dubbing and the ribbing are wound on clockwise. Since a tinsel ribbing serves the dual purpose of providing 'flash' and a protection against the turns of dubbing being broken up by the teeth of fish, the ribbing is best wound on counterwise to the dubbing. Soldier Palmer is a good example of the use of ribbing to protect a wound hackle.

Whip Finish

The most efficient method of finishing a fly is to wind a whip finish. With a little practice this can be completed quickly and neatly by hand. Alternatively, a whip finish tool is obtainable which virtually does the job for you and simple instructions are provided therewith for the uninitiated. Either method is preferable to a series of half-hitches, a knot which is definitely not secure.

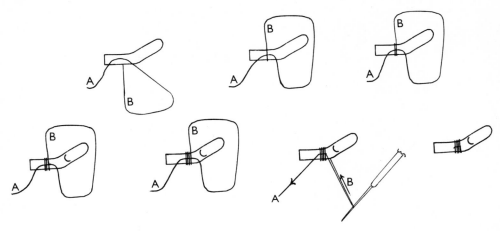

29 *Sequences of the whip finish*

Dyeing

Nature does not provide a range of colours in natural fibres to supply all the subtle variations we seek and it is necessary on occasion to resort to the use of dyes.

Powder dyes are obtainable in a wide range of colours which are easy to use and, provided the maker's instructions are followed in the first stages of experience, will give satisfactory results. Later, as one becomes more experienced, the mixing of two or even more dyes can be experimented with to produce more subtle shades.

Most natural fibres have some oil and this needs to be removed with detergent or a special cleaner manufactured for the purpose, before the material can be dyed. Capes, hackles tied in bunches, primary and secondary feathers, fur and hair can all be treated. See also my comments on picric acid (page 57).

Additional Tips

There are one or two other points I should like to make which may be found helpful. Do not take two turns of silk where one will suffice, nor add a turn to do the job which the previous turn should have been made to do. When deciding how far down the shank the body should end, a good pointer is 'not beyond the point of the barb.'

In fly-tying parlance 'up the shank' means toward the eye and 'down the shank' toward the bend.

Let no-one fear that large hands will prevent the tying of small flies. It has been my happy experience to see such students produce the most exquisite small dry flies. Deficient eyesight can be assisted by the use of a magnifier, some models of which can be attached to the stem of the vice and adjusted for height and angle. Where something more elaborate is sought, an optically ground magnifier with built-in illumination, as used for the inspection of miniature components, can be obtained. This instrument reveals every part of the dressing with great clarity. The magnification is usually pre-set but other models are constructed to provide variation. They are rather expensive at about £75 ($190 USA) as at 1980, but will last for years.

Nothing will clarify the various operations performed in tying flies so much as personal instruction or watching a proficient friend. There are many courses designed for this purpose and personal individual tuition is also available. The next best thing is a book, but a written text alone is not enough. In my experience as an instructor over more than ten years I have learned the benefits to be derived from providing all the relevant detail in sheet form so that the student can follow the same procedures at home as he has done during his instruction. It is this method which I have used for each of the 50 patterns described in this book. Each dressing includes general information on the particular fly, followed by a list and description of the materials set out in order of use, and numbered operations which are supported by similarly numbered line drawings. Options or substitutes are mentioned where relevant. My students assure me that what they have come to call Freddie's hymn sheets or menus are most helpful.

Like riding a bicycle, fly-tying needs only practice. In this respect I advocate that when you have selected the pattern, you tie not one, but at least four and preferably six, examples of the same pattern in one tying session. As each one is completed you will see your errors which you can then remedy in the next example and so on until the perfect result is obained.

In this book I have tried to provide for all levels of proficiency and I hope that I have succeeded. It is said that determination and a spoon will empty the ocean, so press on! There is grand satisfaction in contemplating a fish on the bank which took a fly you tied yourself.

4

Patterns

Wet Flies

1 Alexandra
2 Black and Peacock Spider
3 Black Spider
4 Black Zulu
5 Blue Upright
6 Butcher (or Silver Butcher)
7 Coachman
8 Connemara Black
9 Dunkeld
10 Golden Olive
11 Greenwell's Glory
12 Grouse Series
13 Invicta
14 Mallard and Claret
15 March Brown
16 Partridge and Orange
17 Peter Ross
18 Pheasant Tail
19 Red Tag
20 Snipe and Purple
21 Soldier Palmer
22 Straddlebug Mayfly
   (or Summer Duck)
23 Teal Series
24 Wickham's Fancy
25 Woodcock and Green

Dry Flies

26 Black Gnat
27 Caperer (or Welshman's
   Button)
28 Coch-y-Bondhu
29 Crane Fly
   (Daddy-Long-Legs
30 Gold Ribbed Hare's Ear
31 Grannom
32 Greenwell – hackled
   variant
33 Grey Duster
34 Grey Wulff
35 Hacklepoint Coachman
36 Imperial
37 Iron Blue Dun
38 Large Dark Olive Dun
39 Last Hope
40 Light Cahill
41 Little Dorrit
42 Orange Quill
43 Pale Watery Dun
44 Quill Gordon
45 Red Quill
46 Sherry Spinner
47 Simple Fredsedge
48 USD Para-Olive
49 USD Poly-Red Spinner
50 Walker's Sedge

1   Alexandra

attributed to W. G. Turle

Originally known rather poetically as Lady of the Lake, this fly was renamed after the then Princess Alexandra. It is essentially a lake or reservoir fly, little used on rivers except, perhaps, for sea trout where flash from the silver body may be of benefit.

At one time banned from some waters because of its supposedly killing reputation, its popularity waned but it might be returning to favour, although I suspect this may be due less to its success in the water than to its attractive appearance.

It is best used in cold weather, fished on the point and well sunk, for it seems probable that it was intended to represent small fry such as minnows or sticklebacks. The peacock wing needs to be sleek rather than bushy to achieve the right effect.

Both Alexandra and the Jungle Alexandra have their supporters. The winging material is rather intractible and presents something of a challenge to the fly dresser.

Materials

Hook   Down eye, size 12 or 10 (8 for sea trout)
Working Silk   Black
Tail   Two slips, three to five fibres wide, taken from matching small goose feathers dyed red
Body   Flat silver tinsel
Body Rib   Oval silver tinsel
Beard Hackle   A small bunch of black hackle fibres
Wing   Tips from peacock sword fibres, three to five for each side of the wing
Wing Overlay   A slim slip, red goose, on each side of wing

Tying Operations   (refer to diagrams)

1   Wind on the working silk from behind the eye to the start of the bend where the pair of tail slips and body rib are tied in. Wind working silk back ⅛ in. (3 mm.) from eye.
2   Tie in the silver tinsel for the body and then varnish the turns of silk covering the shank.
3   Whilst the varnish is still wet, wind on the flat body tinsel clockwise in close, tight turns to the joint of tail and back again to behind the eye. Tie off and trim out the surplus tinsel.

4   Pick up the oval tinsel and wind this on anti-clockwise tightly but in open turns to behind the eye. Tie off and trim any surplus oval tinsel.
5   Turn the hook upside down in the vice. Tear out a bunch of fibres from one side of a fairly large black hackle and tie this in as a beard, splaying it slightly. Tie off and trim any unwanted ends at the eye. Turn fly right way up.
6   Select several fibres from each of a left and a right peacock sword quill and tie these in at the eye, back to back, best sides outward, so that they lie as shown.
7A   Cut left and right slips of red goose and place one on each side of the wing. Take two loose turns, adjust for length and then secure and trim any surplus. Whip finish and varnish the whip.
7B   For Jungle Alexandra, carry out operations 1 to 6 inclusive, but then substitute jungle cock feathers for the red goose slips as wing overlay.

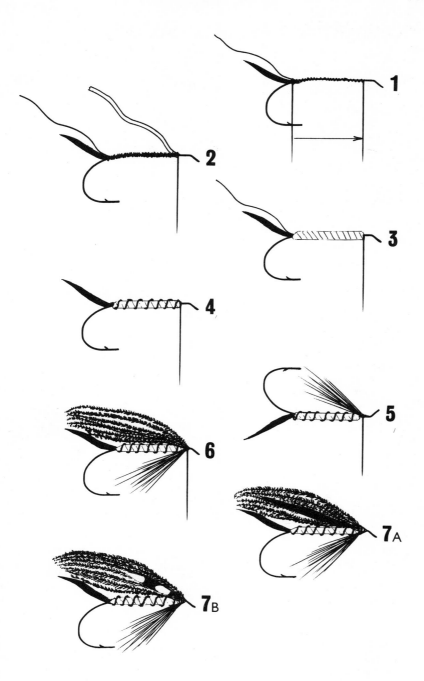

2　Black and Peacock Spider

Tom Ivens

This fly was created by Tom Ivens who brought it to the notice of anglers in his book *Stillwater Fly-Fishing* (1952). The Black and Peacock Spider will take fish under every type of weather condition and in diverse circumstances such as when snails are drifting on the surface or when the fish are beginning to take fry. It will also do well during an evening rise fished on a cast greased down to the last 18 in. so that the fly travels just a little below the surface and *very slowly*. Ivens describes it as a 'deceiver' pattern appealing to the natural feeding instinct seldom dormant in the fish. During bright weather a deep sinking pattern on a fairly long leader of 12 ft. or longer, fished slowly over the bottom, has taken many fish for me.

Materials
Hook　Down eye, sizes 10, 12 or 14 (10 most popular)
Wording Silk　Black
Body　Three or four natural herls from below the eye of a peacock eye feather
Hackle　Black, natural or dyed, soft hen hackle

Tying Operations　(refer to diagrams)
1　Wind on the working silk in close turns from ⅛ in. (3 mm.) behind the eye to the start of the bend.
2　Select the peacock herls and tie these in so that the cut ends lie over the shank but a little short of the eye. This helps to fatten up the body. Then wind the working silk back to ⅛ in. (3 mm.) from the eye tying down the herl ends.
3　Using a dubbing needle as shown, or something similar, coat the shank with varnish or Vycoat. Then move *quickly* on to operation 4.
4　Whilst the varnish is still wet, twist the herls anti-clockwise into a rope.

5　Wind on this rope clockwise in close, tight turns, over the tacky varnished body to where the working silk hangs. Tie off and trim out any herl ends which reach beyond the end of the body.
6　Select the hackle, strip off the fluffy fibres at the base, and tie this in at the eye end so that the flat plane of the hackle is at right angles to the body, the natural bend of the quill leaning backwards towards the bend.
7　Using hackle pliers or fingers, wind on the hackle two or three turns. Then tie off, trim out the surplus hackle tip and butt and add a whip finish which should then be varnished.

Note　I prefer a hackle long in the fibre since this seems to work well in the water, giving an impression of life. A slow bunching of the line in the palm of the hand seems most effective in using this fly. Takes occur at all levels but slowly near the bottom on a long leader does best. Lead or copper wire can be wound on and varnished prior to operation 1 for quick sinking.

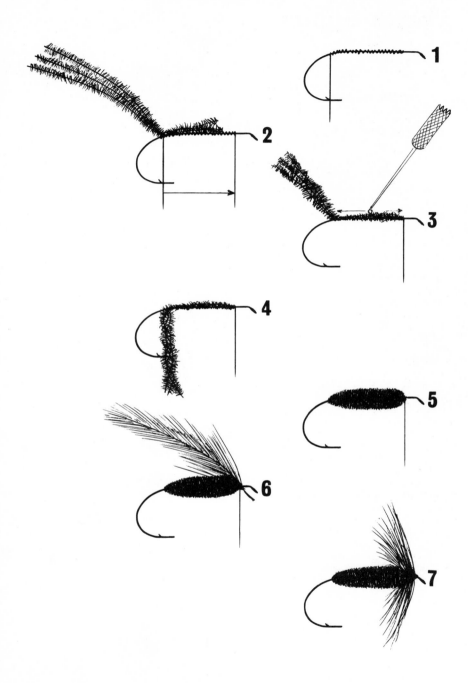

3   Black Spider

James Baillie

For W. C. Stewart, author of *The Practical Angler* (1857), the Black Spider was the most favoured wet fly and, in his opinion, there was no more killing pattern. Stewart had a reputation for catching vast numbers of fish using this fly and is reputed to have had one of these Spider patterns on his cast from the day he first saw it. Useful all year but best in spring, the Black Spider must, as its name implies, be sparsely dressed with a soft hackle so that the movement of the stream will impart life to the fly. The earliest dressing seems to have had a body of brown silk with the familiar hackle from the neck of the starling which has a green sheen to it.

Materials

Hook   Down eye, size 12, 14 or 16
Working Silk   Black
Body   Black silk (occasionally orange or dark red) or a dark peacock quill stripped of its flue
Tip   Optional, but when added is of orange or red floss or silk
Hackle   Black hen or a starling neck hackle with a green sheen

Tying Operations   (refer to diagrams)

1   Wind on the working silk from a little behind the eye to the start of the bend.
2   If an orange or red tip is to be included, tie in a short length of floss at the bend, then wind the working silk slightly towards the eye.
3   Wind on the floss, forming a small tip. Tie off and trim out surplus floss.
4A   If a quill body is your choice, tie in the stripped quill where the silk hangs. Then wind the working silk to just short of the eye.
4B   The quill is now wound on in close, touching turns, to where the silk hangs. Tie off and trim out surplus quill end. If you have decided *not* to incorporate a quill body you can omit instructions 4A and 4B and follow on from instruction 3.

4   Wind on a neat and slightly tapered body of working silk, leaving room at the eye to tie in and wind on the hackle.
5   Select and tie in the hackle where the silk hangs, the flat plane at 90° to the shank and the outer bend facing the eye. Wind the silk to just short of the eye.
6   Wind on the hackle two to four turns at most. Secure, then trim out the remaining hackle tip and butt, wind a neat head completing with a whip finish which should be varnished.

For several years now I have used a spider pattern having a flat gold tinsel tip, a slim body of light green floss and a light red game hackle of three turns behind the eye which does well when fish are topping and tailing.

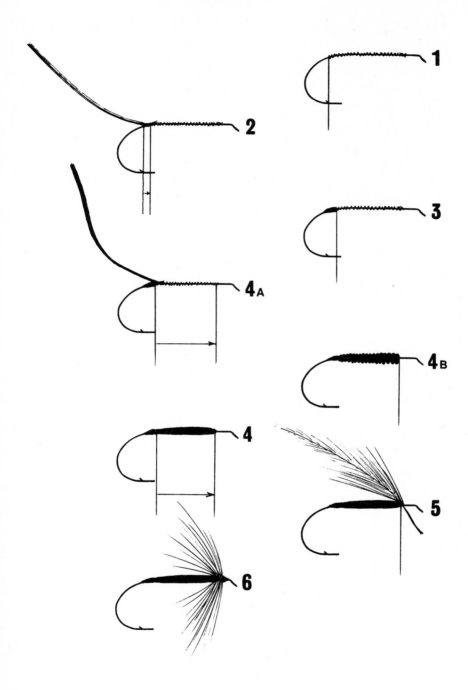

4 Black Zulu

traditional
Little seems to be known about the Zulu which, I suspect, is a variation of a much earlier 'Palmered' fly. Opinion as to its effectiveness differs widely. Some fishermen, particularly in the north, applaud it as a killing fly when used on the top dropper and allowed to skim the surface. Others seem to limit its use to sea-trout waters. Be that as it may, it is a fly that has long been popular in the dressing described below or with a blue hackle either in front of the black or replacing the black entirely. Another variation incorporates black ostrich herl instead of wool for the body, this being more frequently seen in earlier years than now.

For modern reservoir use, two Black Zulus in tandem fished deep and slowly is advocated.

Materials
Hook Down eye, size 14, 12 or 10
Working Silk Black
Tail Originally ibis, now unobtainable, hence paired slips from goose substitute or wool
Body Black wool or seal fur
Body Rib Fine, flat silver tinsel
Body Hackle Black cock

Tying Operations (refer to diagrams)
1 Wind on the working silk in close turns from a little behind the eye to the start of the bend.
2 If using feather, cut matched slips for the tail. If not, cut a short length of red wool. Whichever is used, the tail material is tied in at the bend followed by the ribbing tinsel and if using wool for the body, this also. Operation 3 can then be ignored but wind the silk back to the eye.
3 If using seal fur for the body well wax the working silk and dub on the seal fur.
4 Whichever material is used for the body, wind this on to the position shown. If wool is used, trim surplus.

5 Select and tie in a hackle of appropriate size just behind the eye so that it is at right angles to the shank and with the outside bend facing the eye.
6 Wind the hackle down the body in even turns (Palmerwise) to where the tail joins. Leave the hackle tip in the hackle pliers.
7 Pick up the tinsel and take a tight turn anti-clockwise so that it traps the hackle tip, then continue in open turns up the body four or five turns to where the silk hangs. Tie off, trim out surplus tinsel, hackle tip and butt, wind a neat head finishing with a varnished whip. Finally, using a dubbing needle, release any hackle fibres compressed by the turns of tinsel.

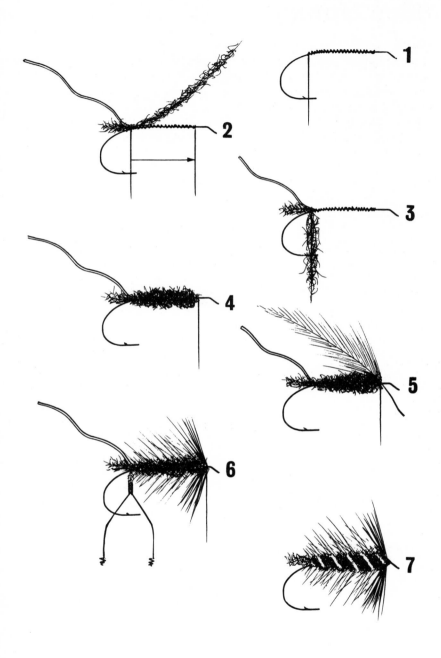

5   Blue Upright

R. S. Austin

A well-known pattern originating in Devon and admirably suited to the rough, fast waters of the area. It is now widely used both as a wet and a dry fly. Austin's pattern is an admirable one for a fly generally representing the dark olive, but a hackle dyed a dark steel-blue must suffice today since the original hackle – nearly black but with a blue centre – is virtually impossible to obtain. The alternative dressing by Skues will serve well for the light olive.

Materials

Hook Up eye for dry, down eye for wet in sizes 12, 14 or 16

Working Silk Purple

Tail Whisks Four fibres from a steel (blue/black) hackle or, for Skues' version, from a pale honey dun hackle

Body A natural peacock herl stripped of its flue to provide a smooth dark quill. One just outside the eye provides a better indication of a segmented body.

Hackle Follow the colouring for tail whisks, a cock hackle for dry, a hen best for wet

Tying Operations   (refer to diagrams)

1   Wind on the working silk in close, tight turns from a little behind the eye to the start of the bend at which point the tail whisks (which some like to point slightly down for dry fly), followed by the stripped quill, are tied in.

2   Wind the working silk back to a little short of the eye forming a smooth, slightly tapered underbody.

3   Varnish the underbody and whilst it is still wet wind on the stripped quill in touching turns to where the silk hangs. Tie off and trim out any surplus quill.

4   Select a hackle to suit the version decided upon and tie it in at right angles to the body, the outer bend of the hackle facing the eye. Leave the silk hanging at the end of the body.

5   Wind on the hackle progressing very slightly towards the eye, four or five turns for dry, two to four for wet. Leave the hackle tip hanging in pliers.

6   Keeping the working silk taut, wind it carefully through the hackle to the eye side where the tip is then secured. Trim out the hackle tip and butt.

7   Wind a neat head and varnish it.

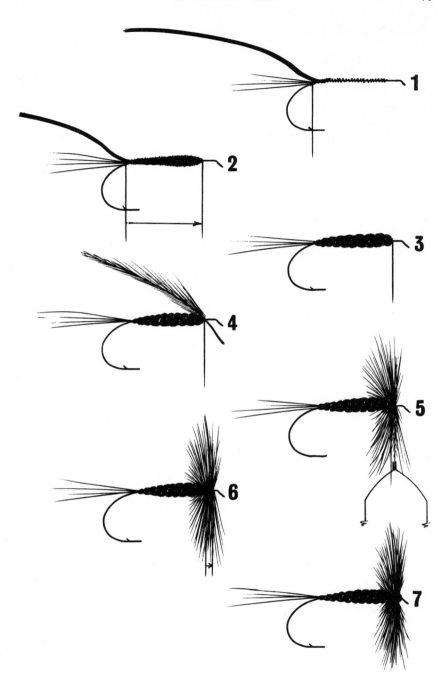

6   Butcher (or Silver Butcher)

Originally the invention of a Tunbridge Wells butcher named Moon, in co-operation with a friend named Jewhurst, also of Tunbridge Wells, this fly was formerly named Moon's Fly and received its present name in the early 1800s. The red tail supposedly represents raw beef and the blue wing the butcher's traditional apron. Could the gleam of the silver tinsel be that of the sharpened knife? Pure conjecture on my part and the name quite probably derives only from Mr Moon's calling. An excellent cold weather fly, the Butcher, fished deep, has saved many a blank day in early spring. Suitable for river, lake or reservoir, it is usually fished as top dropper when using a three-fly leader but I choose to fish it as a single on the point where it seems to excel. Many successful sea trout flies incorporate silver and black and it is due to this, no doubt, that the Butcher is highly regarded for this purpose although, curiously, the Bloody Butcher, which has a scarlet hackle instead of the black, is also esteemed for sea trout.

Materials

Hook   Down eye, sizes 10, 12 or 14; 8 for sea trout
Working Silk   Black
Tail   Paired slips from ibis substitute feathers of a cerise colour
Body   Flat silver tinsel
Body Rib   Oval silver tinsel
Wing   Paired slips from the blue feathers on the outside wing of the mallard drake
Hackle   Black

Tying Operations   (refer to diagrams)

1   Wind on the working silk from a little behind the eye to the start of the bend. Cut a pair of matching slips from ibis substitute feathers, just under 1/8 in. (3 mm.) wide and, placing them back to back so that the natural inside curves face each other, tie them in to extend slightly upwards and beyond the bend as shown. Tie in the oval tinsel, then wind the working silk back to behind the eye.
2   Tie in a short length of flat silver tinsel behind the eye.
3   Wind on the flat tinsel clockwise, edge to edge, to the point where the tail is tied in and then back to where you started. Tie off and trim out surplus tinsel.

4   Pick up the oval tinsel and wind this on anti-clockwise in open turns over the silver body. Tie off at the eye end and trim out surplus oval tinsel.
5   Cut matching slips 1/4 in. (6 mm.) wide from a left and a right blue wing feather and place them back to back, blue sides outward. These are then tied in at the eye end of the body so that they almost reach the tip of the tail. Trim any unwanted ends obscuring the eye.
6   Select a hackle of appropriate size and tie this in at the eye end of the body at right angles to the shank and with the outer bend facing the eye.
7   Wind on the hackle two or three turns, tie off, trim out the hackle butt and tip, wind a neat head completing with a whip finish which should then be varnished.

Note   Operations 6 and 7 show the original form of hackling for the fly, but the modern method is merely to tear out a bunch of hackle fibres from a fairly large hackle and tie it in as a beard at the eye end of the body to project towards the hook point. This is shown in diagram 7A.

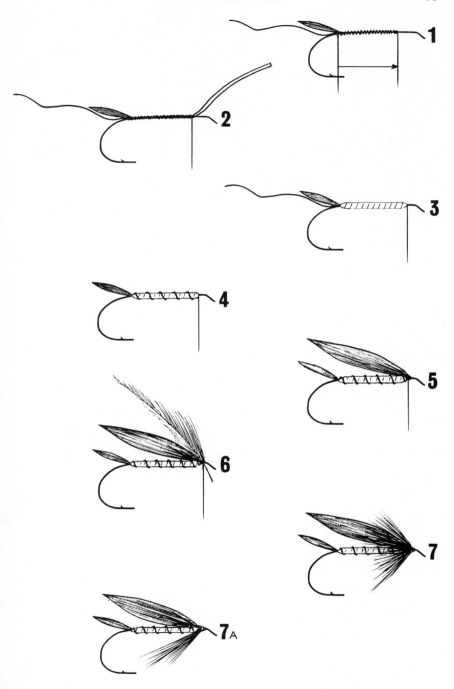

7 Coachman

traditional

Reputed to have been introduced in the early 1800s, the Coachman probably enjoys a greater reputation now than ever before and it can justly be said that any fly still popular after so long and currently used world-wide must have lasting qualities to support its reputation. Although most frequently fished wet it can, on occasion, save the day when fished dry. I find that fished dry it does best in the evening, perhaps because one's concentration can be focused on the white wings but it might be that the somewhat moth-like appearance of the Coachman increases its attraction at that time of day. Fished wet, dull days will, I believe, prove more productive. Precisely who invented the dressing and what it represents, unless it is a fat moth, is somewhat obscure but the Coachman will, I think, earn your praise nevertheless.

For the Lead-wing Coachman it is only necessary to change the wing to coot or waterhen.

Materials

Hook   Down eye generally suffices for both wet (10 to 16) and for dry (14 or 16) but use up eye for dry if preferred

Working Silk   Brown

Body   Three copper-coloured peacock herls from the stem, not the eye

Wings   Paired slips from white undercoverts on the underside of the mallard wing

Head Hackle   Natural red game, cock

Tying Operations   (refer to diagrams)

1   Wind on the working silk from a little behind the eye to the start of the bend.

2   Select the herls from the peacock stem and tie in the cut ends where the silk hangs. Then wind the working silk almost back to where one started behind the eye.

3   Varnish the turns of silk on the shank and whilst it is still wet either wind on the herls as a bunch *or* twist them into a rope and wind this on forming a plumpish body until the working silk is reached. Tie off and trim out the surplus herl ends.

4   Select two matching slips from mallard undercovert feathers. These are then tied in one on each side of the body after the style of a pitched roof, the tips over the bend being slightly higher than at the eye. Trim any surplus wing ends back to behind the eye.

5   Select the red game hackle, not too long in the fibre, and tie this in behind the eye at right angles to the shank with the outer bend facing the eye. Wind the working silk two close turns towards the eye.

6   Wind on the hackle two to four turns without crowding the eye. Tie off, trim out the unwanted hackle butt and tip, wind a neat head and complete with a whip finish which then varnish.

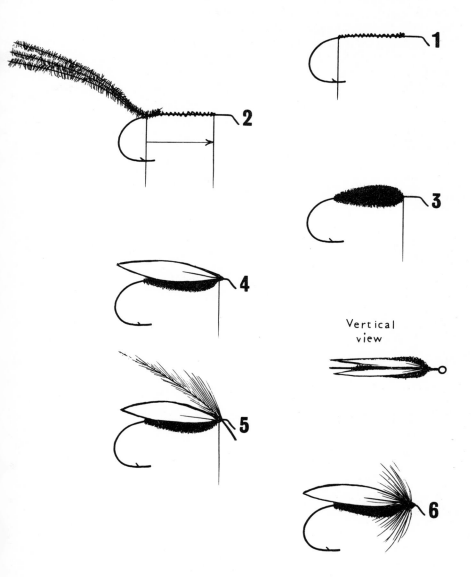

1

2

3

4

Vertical
view

5

6

8   Connemara Black

Little is known of this fly. Originating in Ireland it is naturally an ideal choice for use on the rivers and lakes which abound there, particularly in the west. However, it is perhaps on its reputation as a sea trout fly that its fame has spread far and wide. For this purpose it is much favoured as are many blackish flies showing a touch of silver.

Generally fished on the point, it will do better for sea trout on a partly greased leader or on the top dropper so that it fishes in the surface film or just below.

Materials

Hook   Down eye, size 12, 10 (8 for sea trout)

Working Silk   Black

Tail   Small golden pheasant topping (or crest) feather, pointing upwards

Body   Black seal fur (black wool as substitute)

Body Rib   Fine oval silver tinsel – four turns for size 10, and six for size 8

Beard Hackle   Inner, black cock; outer, blue barred jay

Wing   Slips from bronze mallard shoulder feathers

Tying Operations   (refer to diagrams)

1   Wind the working silk in close turns from a little behind the eye to the start of the hook bend.

2   Tie in the tail feather and the oval tinsel in that order.

3   Well wax the working silk and dub on the seal fur.

4   Wind on the dubbed seal fur forming the body to ⅛ in. (3 mm.) from the eye.

5   Take one turn of tinsel under tail feather to lift it and then wind the tinsel tightly in open turns to the eye end of the body. Tie off and remove any surplus tinsel.

6   Select left and right slips from bronze mallard shoulder feathers and tie these in so that they appear as illustration.

7   Tear out and tie in, as shown, a bunch of black hackle fibres as a beard, for which purpose the fly can, if found helpful, be turned upside down. Then tie in a few blue barred jay fibres over the black beard hackle.

8   Wind a neat head, add a whip finish and varnish the whip. A butt of yellow floss silk is sometimes added before the tail is tied in.

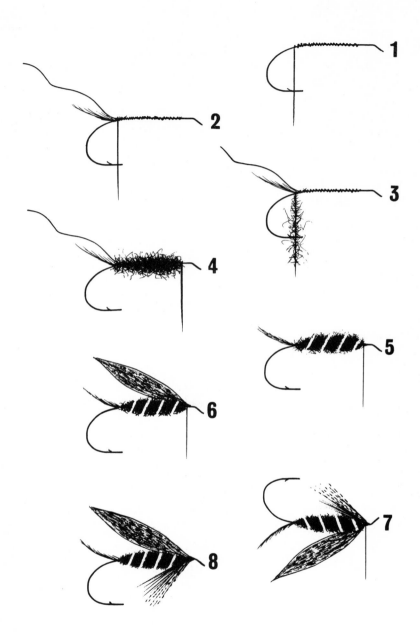

9 Dunkeld

traditional

A scaled-down version of the salmon fly of the same name, the Dunkeld is, as Tom Ivens would describe it, a 'flasher' rather than a deceiver type of fly. I have often heard it described as a 'good-looker' and this may give the angler confidence – so important in trout fishing.

Certainly a touch of orange in a fly is generally considered attractive to the fish and the hackle of this colour, supported by the flash from the gold body and the eye of the jungle cock, may well be a trigger for the trout's predatory instincts. The Dunkeld is fished throughout the season although it is generally most successful in April/May and, whilst commonly fished on the middle dropper, it will do best, I think, on the point and fished fairly deep. It is a popular fly for lakes and reservoirs.

Materials

Hook Wide gape, down eye, 14, 12, 10, 8 (10 and 8 best for sea trout)
Working Silk Brown
Tail Small golden pheasant topping
Body Flat gold tinsel
Body Rib Oval gold tinsel
Hackle Dyed orange hen (or poor grade cock)
Wings Paired slips from brown (termed bronze) mallard shoulder feathers
Eyes Two small jungle cock eye feathers (or substitutes) tied close to the head, one on each side

Tying Operations refer to diagrams
1 Wind on the working silk from behind the eye to the start of the bend at which point tie in the tail topping, natural bend upwards, and the oval gold tinsel. Then wind the silk back to ⅛ in. (3 mm.) from

Tying Operations (refer to diagrams)
1 Wind on the working silk from behind the eye to the start of the bend, tie in the tail topping, natural bend upwards, and the oval gold tinsel. Then wind the silk back to ⅛ in. (3 mm.) from the eye.
2 Tie in the flat gold tinsel and wind this on in tight, touching turns down the shank to the joint of the tail and then back to where you started.
3 Tie in the orange hackle with the outer bend towards the eye.
4 Spiral the hackle down the shank to the tail joint leaving the hackle tip hanging in the hackle pliers.
5 Take one tight turn of oval tinsel round the body in open turns ensuring that the hackle fibres are not compressed. Tie off behind the eye and remove the surplus tinsel and hackle tip and butt.
6 Select and cut out a slip, approximately ³⁄₁₆ in. (5 mm.) wide from each of a left and a right bronze mallard shoulder feather and, placing these back to back, bronze sides outwards, tie these in to lie over the body as in diagram 6.
7 Select two jungle cock eyes of appropriate size and tie one in on each side of the head to lie as shown but avoid spoiling the set of the wings when doing so. The whip finish can then be completed and varnished.

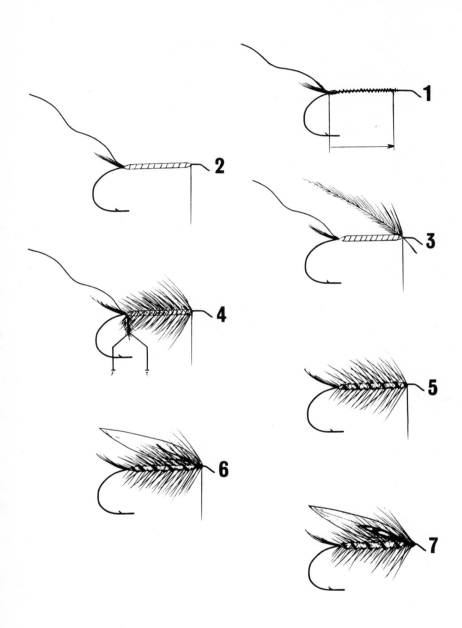

10 Golden Olive

Michael Rogan

This is a variation of the wet fly, Golden Olive, originally developed for Lough Melvin on the borders of north and south Ireland by Michael Rogan's father, a world renowned fly-tyer and designer noted for tying beautiful flies using his fingers as a vice. The original had somewhat elaborate wings of landrail with strips of partridge tail feather along each side. The need for Michael's modification arose from the scarcity of land-rail and his doubt that the required body colour could correctly be obtained by dyeing seal fur in various shades of olive. He found it much more successful thoroughly to mix two separate colours to produce his body dubbing. For the wing he substituted a fairly heavy wing of bronze mallard and changed the original furnace hackle to one of Rhode Island Red. Whereas the original fly was seasonable only from May to July end, the variation produced an all-season fly successful not only on Irish lakes and reservoirs but also on English and Scottish waters. It is best positioned as second dropper on a three-fly leader.

Materials
Hook   Down eye, size 8 or 10, occasionally 12
Working Silk   Golden olive
Tail   Five golden pheasant tippet fibres
Body   Three parts bright yellow seal fur to one part orange seal fur well mixed together as a dubbing
Body Rib   Oval gold tinsel
Wing   Paired slips from bronze mallard flank feathers
Hackle   Rhode Island Red, cock

Tying Operations   (refer to diagrams)
1   Wind on the working silk from a little behind the eye to the start of the bend at which point tie in the tail tippets followed by the body ribbing.
2   Well wax the working silk and dub on the mixed seal fur ready for winding on.
3   Varnish the shank and whilst it is still wet wind on the dubbed seal fur forming the body until just over ⅛ in. (3 mm.) from the eye. Remove any surplus dubbing from the working silk.
4   Pick up the oval tinsel and reverse wind this to the end of the body in four or five open turns. Tie off and remove any surplus tinsel.

5   Cut matching slips approximately ³⁄₁₆ in. (5 mm.) from left and right bronze mallard flank feathers and, placing them back to back, bronze sides outwards, tie them in to lie as shown.
6   Select a hackle the fibres of which, when wound on, will reach the barb and tie this in at right angles to the shank with the outer bend facing the eye.
7   Wind on the hackle two or three turns. Tie off, trim out the hackle butt and tip, wind a neat head and complete with a whip finish which then varnish.

Note   For late season work two turns of a bright claret hackle incorporated before operation 6 will be found profitable, says Rogan.

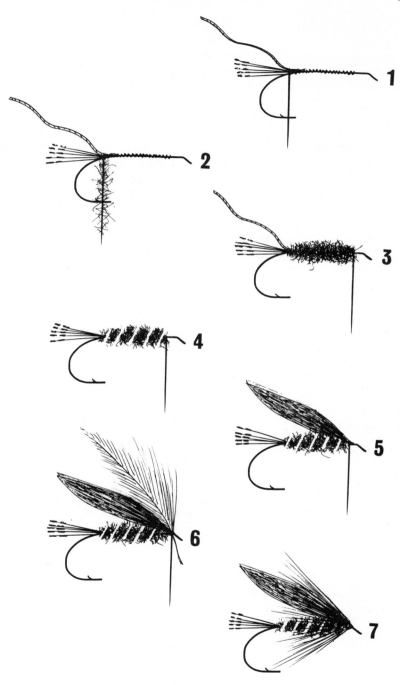

11 Greenwell's Glory

Canon W. Greenwell and James Wright

A world famous and very highly respected fly, Greenwell's Glory originated on the Tweed. In 1854, Canon William Greenwell sought the services of James Wright, a fly-dresser of repute, in producing a dressing which the Canon hoped would prove successful in imitating the fly for which, on his local water, the trout seemed to show preference. Their association perfected the fly, the worth of which Greenwell then proved in the heavy bags of fish he caught with it. As an all-season wet pattern, Greenwell's Glory is almost unrivalled, serving particularly well in appropriate sizes when the Large Dark Olive, Medium Olive or Pond Olive are about. The original dressing called for wings made from a blackbird primary wing feather but since this is no longer used, modern patterns utilise starling, slightly narrower and lighter in colour, without diminishing the taking quality of the fly. Cobblers' wax, a dirty brown in colour, was originally used on the silk to produce the greeny-olive body but is less used nowadays and ordinary fly-tying wax will suffice. The original is best.

For a nymph-suggesting pattern one can do worse in adversity than follow the suggestion made to me by an elderly angler on the Teign in Devon who advocated pinching out most of the wings with one's nails, leaving only stumps.

Materials
Hook Down eye, sizes 12, 14 or 16
Working Silk Primrose or light yellow
Body Working silk, well waxed to appear a dingy olive colour, wound on to form a very slightly tapering body
Body Rib Optional; at one time if a rib was incorporated gold thread was used, but nowadays fine gold wire can be substituted
Wings Matched slips taken from a left and a right starling primary wing feather
Hackle Furnace, a chestnut-coloured hackle with a black centre

Tying Operations (refer to diagrams)
1 Begin by well waxing the working silk. Then wind it on in close turns from a little behind the eye to the start of the bend.
2 Tie in a short length of gold wire where the silk hangs.
3 Wind the working silk back towards the eye forming a very slim, slightly tapered body, but leave adequate room for wings and hackle to be tied in behind the eye.
4 Wind on the gold wire in fairly close open turns to the eye end of the body. Tie off and trim out surplus wire.
5 Cut the wing slips from matched left and right starling wing feathers and, placing them together light sides outward, tie them in to lie as shown. Tie off and trim out any fibre ends over the eye.
6A Turn the fly upside down in the vice.
6B Tear a bunch of fibres from a fairly large hackle and tie it in as a beard at the eye end of the body. Tie off, wind a neat head and complete with the usual whip finish which should be varnished.

In the original a hackle would have been tied in at the eye and wound on two turns.

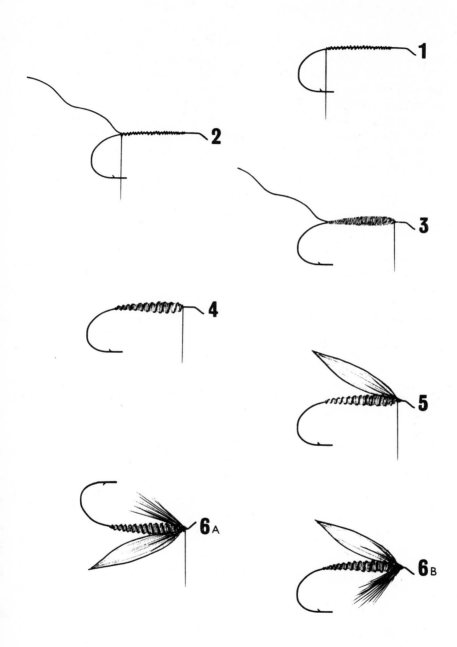

12 Grouse Series

Just who originally developed this series of flies is obscure. Earlier writers merely refer to their northern origin where they were regarded as good general patterns for loch and lake and much thought of for sea trout. The common factor is the Grouse wing but body colours vary considerably being black, brown, green, orange, red, yellow, claret, olive or purple, of which the Grouse and Green, here described, is perhaps the most well known. With the massive expansion of interest in game fishing in recent years and the proliferation of new patterns, the popularity of the Grouse series has declined somewhat though there are many who still favour them. For loch fishing the larger sizes, 10s and 8s, are more usual whereas for lakes and reservoirs 12s and 14s suffice.

Materials

Hook Down eye, sizes 8, 10, 12 or 14
Working Silk Brown
Tail Three or four fibres of bronze mallard shoulder or golden pheasant tippets
Body Green wool or seal fur
Body Rib Gold or silver wire
Wing Paired slips from grouse tail or wing feathers
Hackle Medium to dark natural red game

Tying Operations (refer to diagrams)

1 Wind on the working silk from a little behind the eye to the start of the bend at which point tie in the tail fibres to extend a little beyond the bend as shown.
2 Tie in a short length of wool and the wire at the bend then wind the working silk back in open turns to a short distance from the eye. Varnish these turns of silk.
3 Whilst the varnish is still wet wind on the wool anti-clockwise forming the body finishing where the working silk hangs which is then used to tie off. Trim out any excess wool.
4 Wind on the wire clockwise over the body in four or five open turns finishing at the eye end of the body. Tie off and trim out surplus wire.
5 Cut from grouse tail or wing feathers two matching slips about ¼ in. (6 mm.) wide and place them back to back, darkest sides outward. These are then tied in together at the eye end of the body so that they lie as shown. Tie off and trim out any waste ends at the eye.
6 Select the hackle and tie this in behind the eye at right angles to the shank with the outer bend facing the eye.
7 Wind on the hackle two or three turns, tie off and trim out the hackle butt and tip. Wind a neat head and complete the fly with a whip finish which should be varnished.

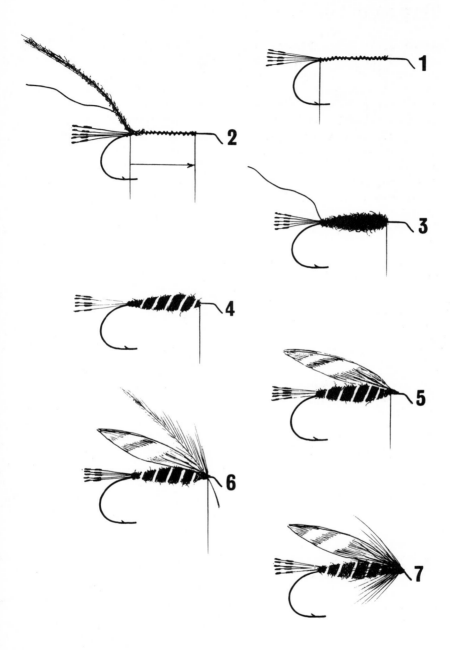

13 Invicta

James Ogden of Cheltenham

The Invicta must be one of the best, if not the best, and most well known of sedge patterns. Devised in the late nineteenth century by James Ogden who had a great reputation as a fly-dresser, this fly has been consistently popular ever since and must have accounted for a vast number of fish. Widely used on the increasing number of reservoirs now given over to trout fishing, it is a fly that takes fish right through the season and when the heavy hatches of sedges appear towards dusk a little later in the season it is a real winner, particularly when fished just beneath the surface when it is taken as a hatching fly. Another successful method during a heavy hatch is to move the fly fairly fast but at a *constant* speed right on the surface of the water to create a wake for which style a leader with a little more strength is a wise precaution. Try it!

Materials

Hook   Down eye, size 14, 12, 10 or 8
Working Silk   Primrose or olive
Tail   A small golden pheasant crest feather
Body   Medium yellow seal fur (wool as substitute)
Body Rib   Qval gold tinsel
Body Hackle   Medium red game or dark ginger cock
Throat Hackle   Blue-barred jay fibres (blue dyed guinea fowl as substitute)
Wings   Left and right slips cut from a hen pheasant centre tail feather

Tying Operations   (refer to diagrams)

1   Wind on the working silk in close, tight turns to the start of the bend.
2   Tie in the crest feather to extend a little beyond the the hook end, then the tinsel.
3   Apply wax to the working silk and dub on the seal fur.
4   Wind on the dubbed seal fur, thin at first then thickening to form a slightly tapered body aproaching the eye; leave ample space for wings and beard hackle.
5   Select the body hackle of appropriate size and tie this in at eye end of the body with the flat plane at 90° to the shank and the outer bend facing the eye.
6   Wind the hackle down the body in open turns clockwise and secure the tip in hackle pliers at the bend.
7   Pick up the tinsel and, with one tight turn, secure the hackle tip then wind the tinsel in open turns up the body, also clockwise, to behind the eye. Tie off, trim the surplus hackle tip at the bend and the tinsel at the eye.
8   Turn the hook upside down in the vice. Tear out a bunch of the blue-barred jay fibres and tie these in with two loose turns. Using a thumb-nail, spread the fibres across the shank and then secure them in that position.
9   Turn the fly right way up in the vice. Select left and right slips of the tail feather of about ³⁄₁₆ in. (5 mm.) width. Place these back to back, best sides outward, and tie them in using the loop method so that the slips just reach the point of the tail. Trim any waste ends over the eye. Wind a neat head finishing with a whip which should then be varnished.

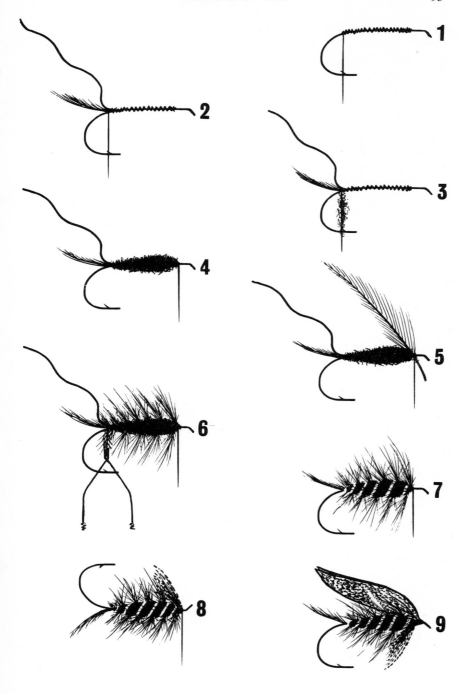

14 Mallard and Claret

attributed to William Murdoch

A fly universally popular and a good general pattern useful throughout the season. To my mind Mallard and Claret is commonly dressed on too large a hook (10s and 8s) which, perhaps supportable on Scottish and Irish lochs, is not so suitable for general use where smaller sizes will be found more telling. It is an ideal fly for those newly introduced to trout fishing whether this be on river, lake or reservoir. For the latter perhaps the most rewarding method is to fish the fly in the vicinity of weed beds but in other circumstances deep rather than shallow and always by slow retrieve.

The Mallard the Claret is said to have originated in Aberdeen and is attributed to William Murdoch who is also credited with the invention of the Heckham Peckham and a number of lake flies now little used.

Materials

Hook Down eye, size 12 or 10 (8 for sea trout)
Working Silk Claret or black
Tail Four to six golden pheasant tippet fibres
Body Claret seal fur or wool; both are illustrated although I prefer seal-fur
Body Rib Oval gold tinsel; fine gold wire suffices for smallest size
Wing Paired slips from left and right bronze mallard shoulder feathers
Hackle Hen, dark red game normal but claret sometimes used

Tying Operations (refer to diagrams)

1 Wind on the working silk from behind the eye to the start of the bend.
2 *If using wool,* tie in the tail fibres, a strand of wool and the oval tinsel, *or*
3 *If using seal fur,* tie in the tail fibres and the oval tinsel. Wax the working silk and dub on the seal fur, thinly at first thickening later.
4 Wind on the wool or seal fur clockwise forming the body. Stop short about ⅛ in. (3 mm.) from the eye. If wool is used, tie off and trim out surplus.

5 Wind on the tinsel anti-clockwise in four to six neat open turns to form the body rib. Tie off and trim surplus tinsel.
6 Cut a slip, 3/16 in. (5 mm.) for size 10 as a guide, from each of a left and a right bronze mallard shoulder feather. Place these back to back bronze sides outward and tie these in behind the eye so that the strips sit vertically on the shank. Trim out any unwanted ends obscuring the eye.
7 Select the hackle, strip off the unwanted fluffy base and tie it in behind the eye at right angles to the body with the outer bend facing the eye.
8 Wind on the hackle two to four turns according to hook size progressing very slightly towards the eye. Tie off, trim out the hackle butt and tip, wind on a neat head and complete with a whip finish which should be varnished.

Note There are variations in dressings. One calls for oval silver tinsel, not gold. Another suggests that the rear half of the body be made up of flat silver tinsel with claret seal fur or wool for the front half.

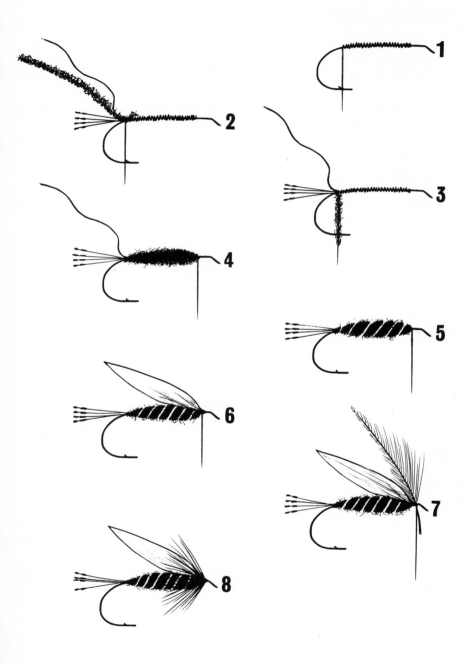

15 March Brown

based on Bowlker, 1747

This is a fly which, over the years, has been subject to a great many variations. It has had wings both of hen pheasant and partridge and dressings were given as long ago as 1681 by Chetham. I have little doubt a pattern existed in Walton's early life. Two species of the natural fly exist, the most common, which hatches in reasonable strength in March/April, being *Rhithrogena haarupi,* the true March Brown, prevalent on Welsh rivers like the Usk and on northern streams but unlikely to be seen in the south. The other is *Ecdyurus venosus,* a larger and lighter coloured fly which appears in less strength mainly in May and June. The March Brown can almost be guaranteed to be seen in flyboxes up and down the country and in use in substantial numbers in the early season. Whether the artificial is, in fact, taken by the trout as the natural or as something else entirely is open to debate but, as G. E. M. Skues wrote, the March Brown 'is an excellent fly, and as generally tied, quite a poor imitation of the natural fly and quite a passable one of almost anything else.' I would only add that in my experience the more nymph-like the pattern the more successful it is.

Materials
Hook   Down eye, size 10, 12 or 14
Working Silk   Brown
Tails   Two fibres from a brown mottled partridge back feather
Body   Hare's body fur
Body Rib   Optional but when used yellow silk
Beard Hackle   A bunch of fibres as for tails
Wings   Paired slips from a left and a right hen pheasant primary wing feather

Tying Operations   (refer to diagrams)
1   Wind on the working silk from a little behind the eye to the start of the bend.
2   Tie in two fibres from a partridge back feather, followed by a short length of yellow silk. Well wax the brown silk and dub on the fur ready for winding.
3   Wind on the dubbed fur thinly at first but thickening somewhat towards the eye. Tie off and remove any surplus fur from the brown silk.
4   Wind on the length of yellow silk in four or five open turns which will tend to sink into the fur. Tie off using brown silk and remove any surplus yellow silk.

5   Turn the fly upside down in the vice. Select a bunch of fibres from the partridge back feather and tie it in as a beard as shown. Trim any hackle ends over the eye.
6   Turn the fly right way up in the vice. Cut matching slips from a right and a left hen pheasant wing primary feather and, placing them back to back, tie them in as shown. Add a small touch of varnish to those securing turns, wind a neat head completing with a whip finish which then varnish.

Note 1   For the Silver March Brown the body is of flat silver tinsel ribbed with oval silver, the tails, wings and hackle unchanged.
Note 2   A useful nymph-like pattern omits the wings and instead of a beard hackle, a long fibred partridge back feather is wound on two turns only. Try it in the early to mid-season.

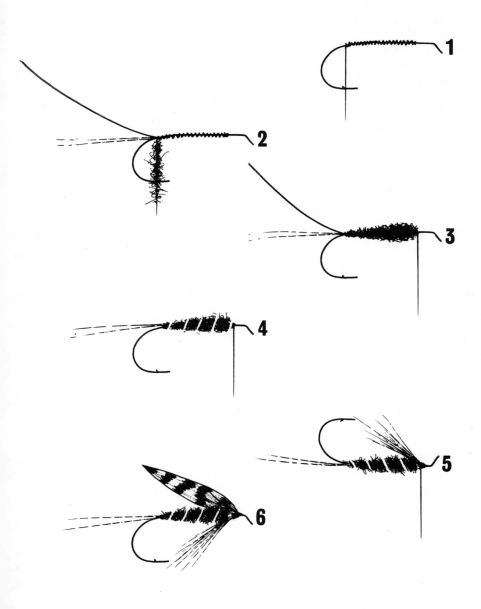

16 Partridge and Orange

traditional

A north country pattern of long standing known at various times as Partridge, Partridge Hackle or Partridge Spider, for the most part dressed without a ribbing of fine gold wire which is a comparatively recent variation. A reliable fly on fairly swift-flowing rocky northern rivers where it is invariably fished wet and by no means to be despised for lake or reservoir. Its success might be attributed to the translucence and rich colour transformation which occurs when the silk body becomes wet, the soft hackle adding life and movement in the play of the current. Of similar patterns employing bodies of black, green, claret or yellow silk, only the latter seems to have retained much popularity. A spider pattern representing a small Stone Fly, the Partridge and Orange is generally regarded as an all-season fly effective for trout and grayling.

Materials

Hook Down eye, size 14
Working Silk Hot orange
Body Working silk as above though some prefer to overlay this with a winding of orange floss silk
Body Rib Optional but, when used, fine gold wire
Hackle A well-dappled feather of brown and buff from the back of a partridge, prepared as in diagrams 'A' and 'B' which are shown a little larger than actual size.

Tying Operations (refer to diagrams)

1 Secure the working silk a little away from the eye, then wind it on in close, neat turns until above the start of the barb.
2 Tie in a short length of fine gold wire at the bend.
3 Wind the silk in neat, level layers back to the starting point, once again back to above the barb and finally back to a little behind the eye, leaving sufficient space for the hackle and final whip.
4 Wind on the gold wire in even open turns to the eye end of the body; secure and trim out surplus wire.
5 Select the partridge hackle – diagram 'A' – and prepare it as in 'B.' It can then be tied in with the best side (the convex or outer bend side) facing the eye.
6 Wind on the hackle two or three turns, each turn progressing very slightly towards the eye. Tie off, trim out the surplus hackle tip and butt and complete with a whip finish which should be varnished.

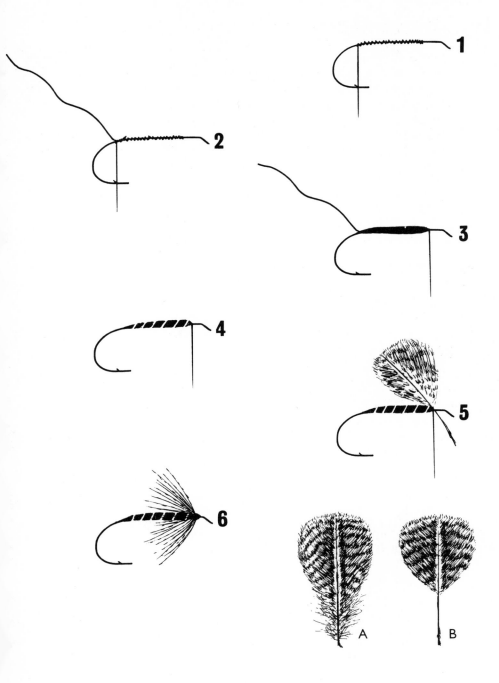

17 Peter Ross

Evolved by Peter Ross of Killin, Perthshire, this fly is a variation of another well-known fly, the Teal and Red. The revised dressing was an immediate success and brought Peter Ross lasting fame. Although he was not a fly-dresser his inspiration produced a pattern which is to be found in almost every flybox at some time. Whilst not so successful as a general river fly, it is renowned for sea trout and it really seems to have come into its own as a reservoir fly, the silver flash, a touch of red up front and the barred wings perhaps giving it a fry-like appearance.

Materials

Hook Down eye, size 12 or 10 (8 for sea trout)
Working Silk Scarlet or black
Tails Four or five golden pheasant tippet fibres
Rear Half Body Flat silver tinsel
Front Half Body Scarlet seal fur dubbed on
Body Rib Oval silver tinsel over both halves of the body
Hackle Black cock hackle fibres tied in as a beard
Wing A slip taken from each of a left and a right teal breast or flank feather

Tying Operations (refer to diagrams)
1 Wind on the working silk from a little behind the eye to the start of the bend.
2 Tear the fibres from the tippet feather and tie these in to lie as shown, avoiding any tendency to make them too long or too short. Follow these with the oval tinsel, then the flat. The working silk can then be wound two-thirds of the way back along the shank.
3 Varnish the turns of silk on the shank and whilst it is still wet wind on the flat tinsel clockwise to where the silk hangs. Tie off and trim surplus tinsel.

4 Well wax the working silk and dub on a little seal fur.
5 Wind on the seal fur in close turns forming the front portion of the body. Remove any unwanted fur remaining on the working silk.
6 Wind on the oval tinsel anti-clockwise over both rear and front body portions. Tie off and trim out surplus oval tinsel.
7 Turn the fly over in the vice. Tear out a reasonable bunch of fibres from a fairly large black cock hackle and tie these in as shown to form the beard. Trim off any ends over the eye and turn the fly right way up.
8 Cut out a matched pair of slips from the left and right teal feathers so that the *inward* bend on each slip is neatly up against the other. These are then tied in to lie as shown. Trim out any unwanted ends at the eye then, ensuring that the vertical set of the wings is not disturbed, wind a neat head and complete with a whip finish which then varnish.

Note Some dressers prefer to tie in the wings before adding the beard hackle. Choose the method most to your liking.

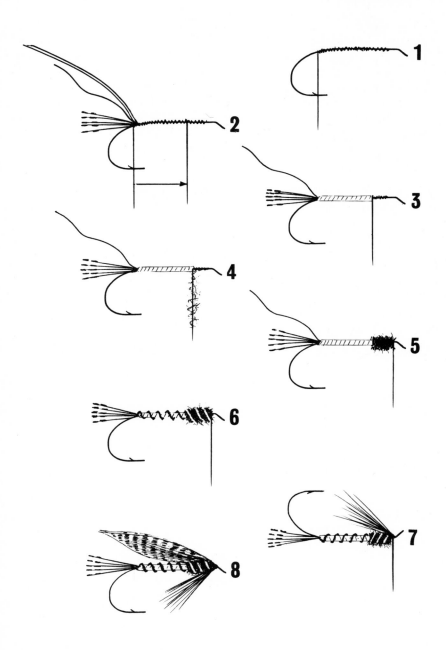

18   Pheasant Tail

Payne Collier

Originating in Devon, the Pheasant Tail is now very widely known and few flies are so well regarded whether for use on lake, reservoir or river, for brown trout, rainbows or grayling. Generally respected more as a spinner pattern than as a dun it is nevertheless fished with effect both wet and dry. As a spinner it is an effective representation of a number of olives, including the Upright, and will equally suffice for the Small Spurwing, Dusky Yellowstreak and the Sepia Dun. As a general pattern it must surely be worthy of a place in the flybox and from May to the season's end can justly be expected to more than earn its keep.

Materials

Hook   Up eye for dry, down eye for wet, size 16 or 14, occasionally 12
Working Silk   Brown
Tails   Two or three fibres from a honey dun spade feather or large hackle, cock, ginger as substitute
Body   Two or three strands from a cock pheasant centre tail
Body Rib   Fine gold wire
Hackle   Honey dun cock, ginger as substitute

Tying Operations   (refer to diagrams)

1   Wind on the working silk from a little behind the eye to the start of the bend.
2   Select and tie in the tail fibres to extend a body length beyond the point of tying in.
3   Tie in a short length of gold wire followed by the pheasant tail fibres. Then wind the working silk back to behind the eye.
4   Varnish the turns of silk on the shank and whilst it is still wet twist the pheasant tail fibres into a rope and wind this on anti-clockwise forming the body. Cease winding where the silk hangs, tie off and trim out the surplus fibre ends.
5   Pick up the gold wire and wind this on clockwise in four or five open turns to the end of the body. Tie off and trim out surplus wire.
6   Select the hackle and tie this in at the eye end of the body at right angles to the shank and with the outer bend facing the eye. Then wind the silk *slightly* towards the eye.
7   Wind on the hackle in three to five close turns progressing towards the eye. Tie off, trim out the hackle butt and tip, wind a neat head completing with a whip finish which then varnish.

Note   A. Courtney Williams comments that for a representation of the Iron Blue a blue dun hackle is the best.

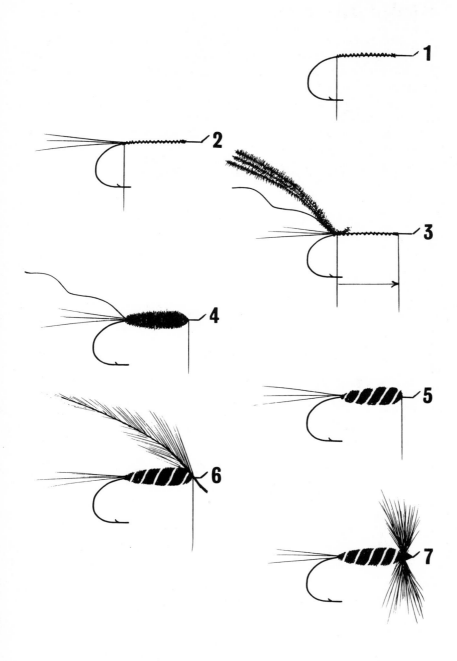

19 Red Tag

A. Courtney Williams suggests that this fly was probably the invention of M. Flynn (c. 1850) and it was at that time known in Worcestershire, where it originated, as the Worcester Gem. It is a successful all-season pattern for trout and, particularly from November to April, for grayling although for the latter many prefer the Orange Tag which is dressed with a tag of orange. It is then commonly called Treacle Parkin, particularly in the north. An intriguing name which surely must have a story attached.

Materials

Hook Up eye for dry fly, down eye for wet fly, size 12 or 14
Working Silk Brown
Tag Currently red wool, but originally a scarlet feather such as ibis
Body Three of four green/bronze herls from below the eye of a peacock feather
Hackle Natural red game, cock for dry, hen for wet

Tying Operations (refer to diagrams)

1 Wind on working silk from a little behind the eye to the start of the bend.
2 Cut a short length of wool and the peacock herls and tie these in together so that they lie over the hook shank with the longest ends overhanging the bend. Wind the silk back to about ⅛ in. (3 mm.) from the eye, binding down the wool and herl ends over the shank.
3 Then varnish these turns of silk.
4 Whilst the varnish is still wet, either twist the herls into a rope, which makes the herls less liable to damage by the teeth of the fish, and wind this on, or wind on the herls in a bunch as they are, the body ending where the working silk hangs. The herls are secured at this point and the excess herl trimmed off. Next, trim back the wool tag so that it is about a quarter of the length of the body.

5 Select the appropriate hackle and cut away the bottom one-third of the fibres leaving a narrow band of cut fibres on both sides of the quill which will assist the silk to grip it. Tie in the hackle securely at the eye end of the body, the flat plane of the hackle at 90° to the shank and the outer bend facing the eye.
6 Leave the working silk hanging at the eye end of the body. Then, using hackle pliers or fingers, wind on the hackle three or four turns towards the eye and leave the hackle tip hanging in the hackle pliers.
7 Keeping the working silk *taut*, wind it through the hackle to behind the eye, separating the hackle fibres if necessary with a dubbing needle as you go. Tie off, trim out the tip and butt end of the hackle. To complete the fly, wind a neat head and add a whip finish which should then be varnished for security.

Note Whenever a hackle is to be tied in and wound on the method of preparation described in stage 5 above will be found helpful.

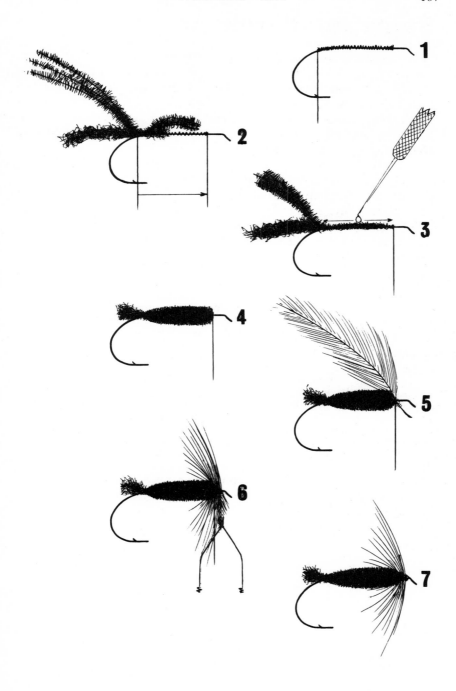

20 Snipe and Purple

A wet pattern more generally used in Yorkshire and the north than else-where it is claimed to represent both the Iron Bue Dun (*Baetis pumilus or B. niger*) and the Small Dark Olive (*Baetis scambus*) although not everyone agrees. It is a useful pattern for ruffled streams usable through much of the season though possibly best in May and August and again in late September and October for both trout and grayling. Whilst usually fished singly on the point another can be added on the bob.

The hackle required is found on the outside of the snipe's wing (uppermost in flight) near to the centre elbow joint, and is described by A. Courtney Williams as 'a dark feather, nearly black.' However, in the many wings I have examined the darkest is at best a dark grey/brown, the outer edges of the tip being fawn. Since this is a spider type of fly the hackle needs to be worked upon by the current and the fly should there-fore be sparsely dressed.

Materials
Hook Down eye size 14 or 16
Working Silk Purple
Body Purple floss silk
Hackle See general description above

Tying Operations (refer to diagrams)
1 Wind on the working silk from a little behind the eye to the start of the bend.
2 Tie in a short length of floss silk as shown, then wind the working silk back in close tight turns to behind the eye, leaving room to wind the hackle. Varnish the turns of silk on the shank.
3 Whilst the varnish is still wet, wind on the floss silk flatly to give a smooth, slim, slightly tapering body thickest near the eye. Tie off and trim out surplus floss.
A, B. Select the hackle to be used from the snipe wing as shown in 'A.' Strip off the lower fibres as in 'B' ready for tying in.

4 Tie in the hackle at the eye end of the body.
5 Wind on the hackle, two, or at most three, turns progressing towards the eye then take one turn of silk through the hackle to just behind the eye and secure the hackle tip. Trim out the hackle tip and butt, wind a neat head and complete with a whip finish which then varnish.

Note Others in the Snipe series are the Snipe and Yellow and the Snipe and Orange for which only a change in the colour of the working silk and body floss is necessary. They provide useful alternatives to the Purple and are fished in the same way and in the same periods of the season.

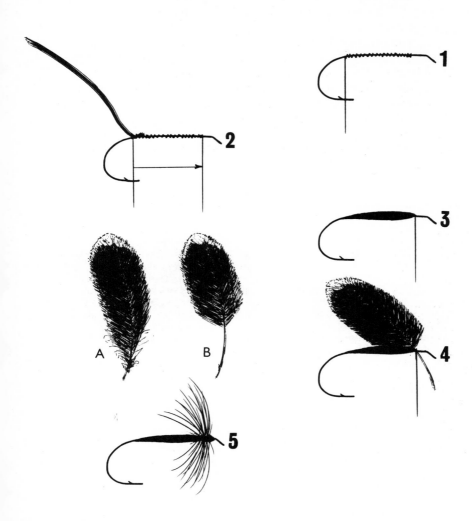

21 Soldier Palmer

traditional

The name Palmer is said to have been applied to the returning pilgrims who brought fronds of palm with them from the Holy Land. These fronds are somewhat similar in appearance to hackles, much enlarged, and it might well be that the Palmer was so named because of this similarity. It is mentioned in the second edition of *The Boke of St Albans* (1496) and by Walton and Cotton later. To some early anglers the Palmer was supposedly a representation of the hairy type of caterpiller but this seems doubtful, although I believe there is a moth whose caterpillar feeds on the bankside alder. The Soldier Palmer, here described, may have been named after the English Redcoats. There are other Palmer patterns, notably Black, Red and Grey, less used now than of yore, all of which can be fished wet or dry.

Materials

Hook   Up eye for dry, down eye for wet, sizes 10 to 16
Working Silk   Scarlet
Tail and Body   Scarlet wool
Body Rib   Fine flat gold tinsel
Hackle   Medium red game, cock

Tying Operations   (refer to diagrams)

1   Wind on the working silk from behind the eye to the start of the bend. Tie in the tinsel, then the wool, leaving a small wool tail about ⅛ in. (3 mm.) long protruding beyond the bend. Then wind the working silk back to a little short of the eye.
2   Varnish the turns of silk on the shank and whilst it is still wet wind on the wool anti-clockwise until the working silk is reached. Tie off and trim out the surplus wool.
3   Select and tie in the red game hackle at right angles to the shank with the outer bend facing the eye.
4   Wind on two turns of hackle clockwise behind the eye, then further *open* turns down the body until the end of the body is reached. Leave the hackle tip hanging in the hackle pliers.
5   Pick up the tinsel, take one secure clockwise turn at the bend to trap and secure the hackle tip, then wind the tinsel in open turns over the body to the eye, ensuring that the body hackle fibres are not depressed. Tie off, trim out the hackle tip at the bend and the butt at the eye. Wind a neat head completing with a whip finish which then varnish.

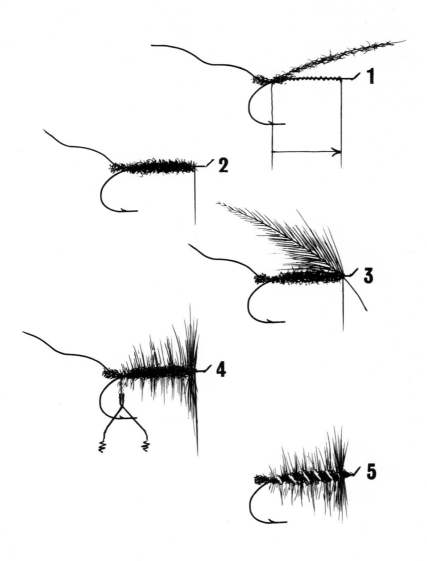

22 Straddlebug Mayfly

otherwise known as the Summer Duck (G. E. M. Skues)

Of all the flies which inhabit our waters surely none has so excited the imagination of the angler or has had more written about it than the Mayfly, of the *Ephemeroptera* order. There are three species of this order found in these islands – *E. danica,* the most commonly seen, *E. vulgata,* less so, and *E. lineata* which is comparatively rare and, in consequence, not of great importance to the angler. Round about the turn of the century some tremendous hatches took place heralding the 'Duffer's Fortnight,' a period when even the beginner could hardly go wrong. Alas, the Mayfly is no longer seen is such quantity and on many waters it is hardly seen at all where previously it flourished. Artificial Mayfly patterns abound but those artistic creations of yesteryear which incorporated fan wings of mallard breast, so much admired in the flybox were, I venture to suggest, not greatly esteemed by the trout though they were fine as fly-tying exercises. A more practical dressing is required and I offer a fairly straight-forward pattern evolved by that master of the chalk stream, G. E. M. Skues, which I think will find favour now as it has in the past. It can be fished sunk, semi-submerged or dry.

Materials

Hook   Long shank, fine wire, Mayfly, size 10 or 12
Working Silk   Brown
Tail   Three fibres from a large black cock hackle
Tip   The original had gold thread but oval gold tinsel will suffice
Body   A thin folded strip of natural raffia as used by gardeners
Body Rib   Brown working silk
Inner Hackle   Hot orange, cock
Outer Hackle   Summer duck originally but now mallard flank dyed buff
Head   One or two natural peacock herls

Tying Operations   (refer to diagrams)

1 Wind on the working silk from a little behind the eye to the start of the bend at which point tie in the tail fibres and the tinsel. The working silk is then wound slightly towards the eye.
2 Wind on the tinsel in three or four close turns forming the tip. Tie off and trim out any surplus tinsel. Next, select a strip of raffia, fold it along its length to give a neat edge and tie it in on the eye side of the tip. Then varnish the shank.

3 Whilst the varnish is still wet, wind on the folded strip of raffia in edge to edge turns forming the body. Secure the end in hackle pliers temporarily.
4 Pick up the silk left hanging at the bend and wind this on in open turns to the eye end of the body.
5 Select the inner hackle and tie this in at right angles to the shank with the outer bend facing the eye.
6 Wind on the hackle in two or three close turns. Tie off and trim out surplus hackle tip and butt.
7 Take a medium-size mallard feather and with the outer bend facing away from you, strip out the fibres from the left side (right side for left-handed fly-tyers). The feather is then incorporated as for the inner hackle in stage 5 above.
8 Wind on the outer hackle in two or three close turns, tie off and trim out the tip and butt. Then tie in one or two peacock herls behind the eye.
9 Wind on the peacock herls forming a ball. Tie off and trim out the surplus herl ends. Wind a neat head completing with a whip finish which then varnish.

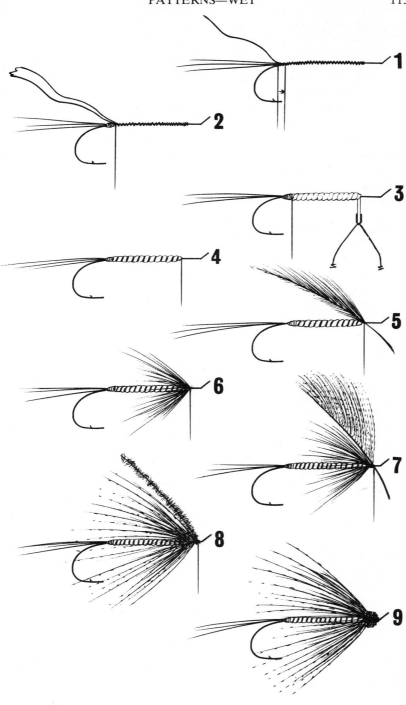

23 Teal Series

traditional
Teal Blue and Silver described
   The series probably started with a single fly in which slips from teal flank feathers were incorporated as wings, the black and white barred effect of the fibres perhaps representing the small scales of fish fry. No doubt, having produced such a fly with a body of a particular colour, the inventor (or others) subsequently rang the changes by varying the colour of the body material, the wing remaining constant. Earlier books on fly-tying describe a range of body colours but at some time there was introduced a variation having a silver body of flat tinsel with a blue hackle – the Teal Blue and Silver – which proved more successful than most of the others. It has maintained its popularity, particularly as a sea-trout fly though the other patterns in the series still have their adherents. The flies in the Teal series, apart from Teal Blue and Silver, have bodies of dubbed seal fur or wool overwound with oval silver tinsel. The various body colours are red, green, yellow, claret, olive, orange and black. The Teal and Black is a popular loch fly and a particular favourite on loch Awe.

Materials
Hook Down eye, sizes 14, 12 or 10, 8 for sea trout
Working Silk Black
Tail Golden pheasant tippet fibres
Body Flat silver tinsel
Body Rib Oval silver tinsel
Wing Paired slips from teal flank feathers
Hackle Cock, dyed teal blue

Tying Operations (refer to diagrams)
1 Wind on the working silk in close turns to the start of the bend where the tails are then tied in.
2 Cut a short length of oval silver tinsel and tie this in at the tail joint. Then wind the silk back to a little behind the eye.
3 Cut a short length of flat silver tinsel and tie this in where the silk hangs.
4 Varnish the turns of silk on the shank then wind the tinsel in touching turns down the shank to the tail joint and back again to where you started. Tie off and trim out any surplus tinsel.
5 Pick up the oval tinsel and wind it tightly over the body in four or five open turns. Tie off and trim out surplus.

6 Select a fair sized hackle dyed teal blue and remove a good bunch of the longest fibres from it. Turn the fly upside down in the vice and tie in these hackle fibres as a beard at the eye end of the body. Trim out the waste ends of the hackle fibres over the eye and then turn the fly right way up.
7 Cut a slip from each of a left and a right teal flank feather, place them back to back and tie them in to lie as shown. Trim any waste end at the eye. Wind a neat head completing with a whip finish which then varnish.

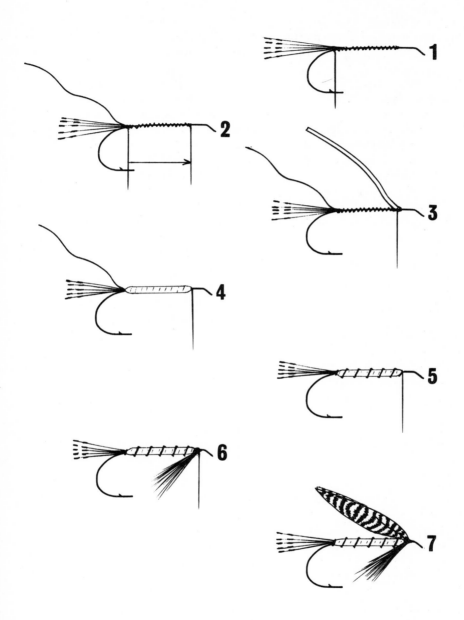

24 Wickham's Fancy

Whether this fly originally came into being as the brain child of Dr J. C. Wickham for whom it was tied by Hammond of Winchester, or of Captain John Wickham, is now unlikely to be resolved, but I lean towards the former for Captain Wickham's pattern had amber coloured silk showing between the ribs of tinsel whereas the fly generally recognised as the Wickham omits it. Just which natural fly, if any, it was intended to represent is unknown and perhaps the only clue is that, according to Hammond, the fly developed an olive tint when placed in the water. Could it then be for one of the olives? Dubious, perhaps, but over the years it has taken countless fish. I remember taking a heavy limit bag with it in a very short time at Grafham Water the year after it opened as a fishery in 1967. It is a most useful pattern throughout the season, more usually fished wet these days, but dry by some for which the wings are vertical or can be omitted altogether. An olive hackle is sometimes substituted.

Materials
Hook   Up eye for dry, down eye for wet, size 14 or 16
Working Silk   Brown or sherry spinner
Tails   Three or four fibres from a ginger or brown cree cock hackle; the original used guinea fowl dyed brown-red
Body   Flat gold tinsel or Lurex
Hackle   Ginger or light red game, cock, wound Palmerwise
Rib   Fine gold wire
Wings   Paired slips from starling primary wing feathers

Tying Operations   (refer to diagrams)
1 Wind on the working silk in close turns from a little behind the eye to the start of the bend.
2 Tie in the tail fibres followed by the gold wire. Then wind the working silk back to where you started in operation 1.
3 Tie in a short length of flat tinsel.
4 Wind on the tinsel in tight turns to the joint of the tails and then back to where you started. Tie off and trim out any surplus tinsel.

5 Select and tie in the hackle at the eye end of the body at right angles to the shank and with the outer bend facing the eye.
6 Varnish the tinsel body and when it is almost dry wind on the hackle in open turns to the tail joint and leave the tip hanging in the pliers.
7 Pick up the gold wire and wind this on (the opposite way from that used for the hackle) first trapping the hackle tip and then progressing in open turns to the eye end of the body. Tie off, trim out the hackle tip and butt, then any surplus wire.
8 Cut a slip from each of a left and a right primary wing feather, place them together so that the tips are level and, for the wet fly, tie them in as shown. Trim out any stumps over the eye, wind a neat head and complete with a whip finish varnished for security.

For the dry fly the wings are usually set in vertically and separated with a figure-of-eight tying.

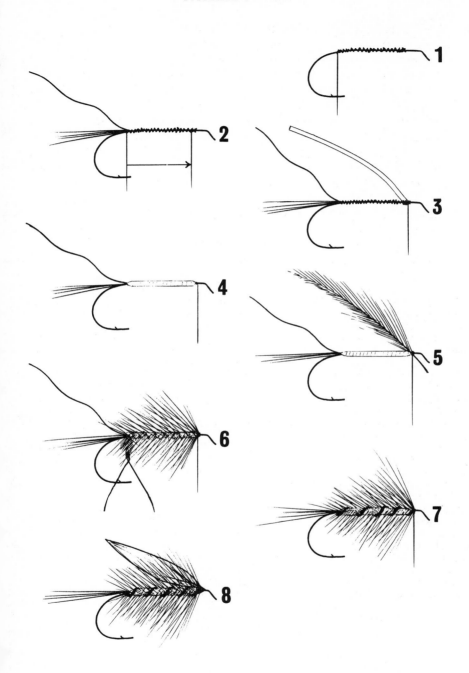

25 Woodcock and Green

traditional

There are series of patterns based upon the winging materials, these being woodcock, teal, mallard and grouse. Perhaps less popular now than formerly they are all standard wet fly patterns originally generally recommended for fishing lakes although all are satisfactory sea-trout flies and were more widely used in the Midlands and north of England than elsewhere. Once one has the Woodcock and Green tying clear one can ring the changes on the Woodcock series and for this purpose I have also described the requirements for the Red and Yellow patterns. My own experience is that they do best in early spring before the water has really warmed up, except the Yellow which, in small sizes, can continue in use up to early June.

Materials

Hook   Down eye, size 14, 12, 10, occasionally 8

Working Silk   Of a colour similar to chosen body colour

Tail   Four fibres from a golden pheasant tippet feather

Body   Green seal fur or fibres of wool, dubbed on

Body Rib   Silver wire or oval silver tinsel, usually the latter

Wings   A slip from a left and a right wing quill of a woodcock

Hackle   Either ginger or dyed green

Note   For Woodcock and Red change the body colour to red and the hackle to natural dark red game.

For Woodcock and Yellow change the body colour to yellow and the hackle to either natural medium red game or dyed yellow.

Others include Hare's Ear, black or orange bodies.

Tying Operations   (refer to diagrams)

1   Wind on the working silk in close turns from a little behind the eye to a point above the barb.

2   Strip out the tippet fibres and tie these in at the start of the bend, together with a short length, say 2 in. (50 mm.), of wire or tinsel.

3   Wax the working silk and dub on a small quantity of seal fur or wool fibres stripped from a length of fine knitting wool.

4   Wind on the dubbed seal fur or wool in close, tight turns forming the tapered body and tie off. Ensure that you leave ample room for the wings and hackle.

5   Wind the wire or tinsel in open turns to the eye end of the body. Tie off and trim out surplus tinsel.

6   Cut out the left and right wing slips approximately ³⁄₁₆ in. (5 mm.) wide for hook size 10 and, placing them back to back, best sides outward, use the loop method to tie them in at the end of the body so that they lie as shown. Trim off.

7   My preference is for a wound hackle (but see 6A below) which I select so that the fibres where the hackle is tied in are just a little shorter than the length of the body. The natural bend of the hackle is towards the tail with the outer bend facing the eye.

8   Wind on the hackle two to four turns according to your preference for a lightly hackled or heavily hackled fly and tie off. Trim out the butt end and the unused tip, wind a neat head and complete with a whip finish which should be varnished.

Option see 6A   Some prefer to tie in a beard hackle for simplicity and speed of tying rather than wind on a full hackle. To do this strip a bunch of fibres from a *large* hackle of appropriate colour and, after turning the fly upside down in the vice, tie in the beard so that it appears as shown in diagram 6A. Trim out the unwanted ends over the eye and complete with a varnished whip.

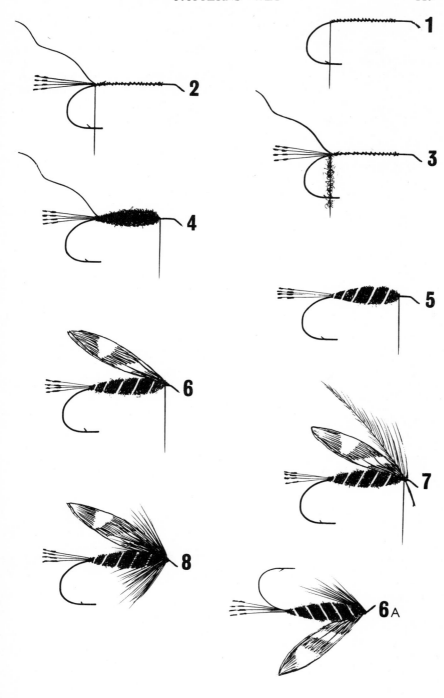

26 Black Gnat

Freddie Rice

The fly to which this general name has been applied is a flat-winged fly (*Diptera*) common in many parts of the country. Of the several species it might represent, perhaps the most important is *Hilara maura* especially on the River Usk where it abounds and which, in May, can be seen swarming up and down above the stream. The Black Gnat, of one species or another, is readily accepted by the trout, particularly in mating pairs which fall on to the surface. It is to be seen on the water at almost any time during the angler's season, hence a pattern or two in the flybox, together with some representative mating pairs, is sound policy. The set of diagrams 'A' to 'E' shows the tying operations for the mating pair.

Materials

Hook Up eye, size 16
Working Silk Black
Body Formed slim, with layers of wound working silk
Body Rib Optional but, when used, fine silver wire
Wing One dozen or so light blue dun hackle fibres
Hackle Starling breast or black cock, natural or dyed

Tying Operations (refer to diagrams)

1 Secure the working silk a little away from the eye and then wind this on in close, even turns down the hook shank to a position above the barb.
2 Wind the silk in close turns back and forth between bend and eye forming the slim body, finishing a little short of the eye.
3 Pull the required number of fibres from the centre portion of a fairly large light blue dun hackle and, laying them over the shank with the torn ends over the eye, secure them in that position. Take one extra turn of silk round the fibres only, followed by one turn round the hook shank. Now is the time to do any adjustment in wing length before using a dubbing needle to apply a very small globule of varnish to the turns securing the wing fibres. Immediately after the varnish has been applied, compress the wing fibres down on to the hook shank, which should splay them to some extent on either side of the fly body. Complete the wing by trimming off the fine tips and remove the butt ends at the eye leaving room for the hackle.
4 Select a hackle and tie this in close to the eye end of the body with the convex side facing the eye.
5 Wind on the hackle three to five turns ensuring that as each turn is taken existing fibres are not compressed. Tie off, trim out surplus hackle tip and butt and add the final whip finish which should be varnished.

Mating Pairs (Diagrams 'A' to 'E')
This dressing calls for two hackles of the same type described for Black Gnat, the one at the eye a little longer in the fibre than that at the bend. The body is similarly made up of wound working silk. No wing.

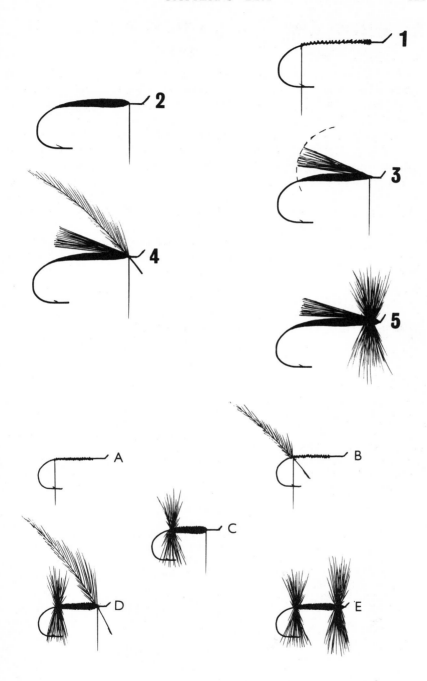

27   Caperer (or Welshman's Button)

W. J. Lunn

One of the most widely known sedge flies, Caperer was produced to imitate a species known as *Halesus radiatus*. The name supposedly comes from the habit of the female to fly in a rising and falling, or capering, motion over the water as she deposits her eggs. A somewhat similar sedge fly, *Sericostoma personatum,* bears the name Welshman's Button applied to it by F. M. Halford, an experienced angler/entomologist, and his application of this name which is generally considered as describing a small beetle, has puzzled anglers for years. The two names, Caperer and Welshman's Button, have become inextricably confused over the passage of time and thus misused. William Lunn, a renowned river keeper on the Houghton Water and an inventive fly-dresser, produced the dressing described below. On high summer evenings when the wind falls off and calm prevails a hatch of sedges will begin and if it is, as it can be, a prolific one, good sport will result, despite the fact that it is hardly a sedge-looking fly.

Materials
Hook   Up eye, 14 or 12
Working Silk   Brown or crimson
Rear Body   Five fibres from a dark turkey tail feather
Ring   Two fibres from a swan's feather dyed yellow
Front Body   As rear body
Rear Hackle   Black, cock
Front Hackle   Medium Rhode Island Red, cock

Tying Operations   (refer to diagrams)
1   Wind on the working silk from behind the eye to the start of the bend, at which point the five turkey tail fibres are tied in. Then wind the working silk ⅛ in. (3 mm.) towards the eye. Varnish the hook shank.
2   Twist the turkey fibres together and wind these over the wet varnish for just under ⅛ in. (3 mm.) towards the eye. Take two turns to secure. Leave the ends of the turkey fibres protruding over the eye.

3   Tie in the two swan fibres. Then wind the working silk about ¹⁄₁₆ in. (2 mm.) towards eye, tying down the turkey fibres as you go.
4   Wind on the swan herls to form a narrow band 2 mm. wide. Tie off and trim the excess swan fibre. Then wind the working silk to within ⅛ in. (3 mm.) of the eye.
5   Wind on the turkey tail fibres to where the silk hangs. Tie off and trim the excess turkey fibres.
6   Select the black cock hackle and tie this in at the end of body with the outer bend facing the eye.
7   Wind on the hackle two-and-a-half turns then tie off and trim the excess hackle.
8   Select the Rhode Island Red hackle and tie this in at the eye in the same manner.
9   Wind on the Rhode Island Red hackle two-and-a-half turns. Tie off, trim out the surplus hackle butt and tip, wind a neat head and add a whip finish. Varnish the whip.

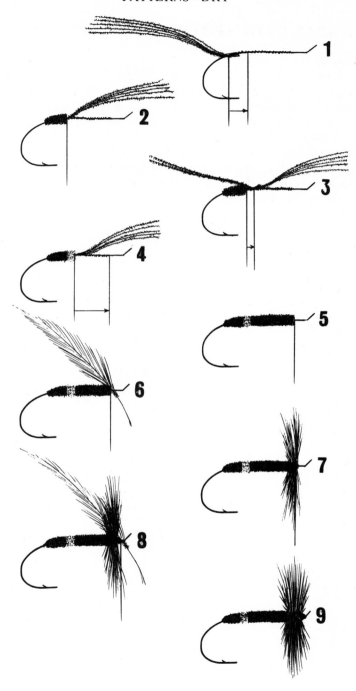

28 Coch-y-Bondhu

traditional

This pattern appears to have been based on a Welsh prototype, possibly *Phyllopertha horticola,* a beetle somewhat less than half an inch in length which has wing cases of reddish brown, a dark peacock green thorax and black legs which could account for the name which might be a corruption of 'coch-y-bonddu' roughly meaning red and black or, as one writer suggests, 'coch-y-boldu' meaning red and black belly. Whatever its origin I have found it kills well in many parts of the country, particularly in Devon waters where a dry pattern on a 14 or 16 hook has, for me at least, risen brown trout over many years during May/June and September. It is a fly I would fish with confidence on a river new to me.

Materials

Hook Up or down eye, size 12, 14 or 16

Working Silk Black or brown

Tag Fine flat gold tinsel or Lurex

Body Three or four bronze peacock herls

Hackle Coch-y-bondhu (furnace as substitute), cock for dry fly, hen for wet fly

Tying Operations (refer to diagrams)

1 Wind on working silk in close turns from behind the eye to the start of the bend at which point tie in a short length of tinsel for the tag. Then wind working silk slightly towards the eye.

2 Form the tag with two or three close turns of tinsel. Tie off and trim out the surplus tinsel.

3 Tie in the peacock herls, cut ends towards the eye. Then wind the working silk to behind the eye, covering the herl ends as you go.

4 Varnish the shank and whilst it is still wet twist the herls into a rope.

5 Wind on the rope in close, touching turns to where the silk hangs. Secure it there and trim off the unwanted herl ends.

6 Select a well-marked hackle of appropriate size and tie this in at the eye end of the body, leaving room to wind it on, the silk to remain on the body side.

7 Wind on the hackle four to six turns, progressing slightly towards the eye, ending with the hackle tip secured in the hackle pliers.

8 Keeping the working silk *taut,* wind it through the hackle to just behind the eye, ensuring that the hackle fibres are not compressed, and secure the tip. Then trim out the hackle tip and butt and complete with a whip finish which should be varnished.

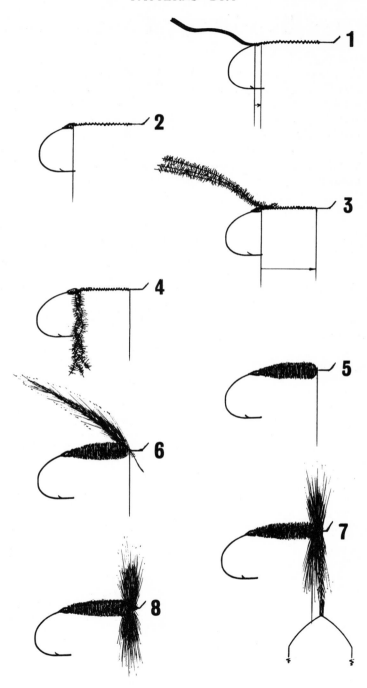

29 Crane Fly (Daddy-Long-Legs)

Richard Walker

These ungainly flies appear to have difficulty in carrying the weight of their bodies whilst in flight and are, in consequence, frequently driven on to the water in even a light breeze. Compared with smaller flies, the Daddies must, because of their size, present an appetising tit-bit to the trout and when they fall the fish are not slow to react to this bounty. Dapping with the natural fly is a favourite method used on Irish loughs and on a breezy day dapping is well worth attempting on any reasonably stocked lake for which, of course, a floss 'blow-line' is called for. This fly is always fished dry. July is the time.

Materials

Hook Long shank, down eye, size 10 or 12, fine wire
Working Silk Sherry spinner
Body Four to six cinnamon turkey tail fibres
Legs Eight cock pheasant centre tail fibres
Wings Ginger cock hackle points
Hackle Ginger cock

Tying Operations (refer to diagrams)
1 Wind on the working silk from behind the eye to the start of the bend.
2 At this point the body fibres are tied in, fine points towards the eye. Then wind the working silk back to ⅛ in. (3 mm.) from the eye.
3 Varnish the shank and wind on the body fibres in close turns towards the eye. Tie off and trim surplus fibre ends.
4 Cut out the cock pheasant tail fibres and tie a knot in each approximately ½ in. (12 mm.) from the fine tip. These are the legs and are tied in by the cut ends four on each side at the eye end of the body so that they trail evenly alongside the hook bend.

5 Select the hackle points for the wings and secure these on top of the shank at the eye end of the body so that they lie flat over the body. Then separate them so that they point diagonally outward at their tips and secure them in that position with figure-of-eight turns.
6 Select two hackles of appropriate size and tie these in at the eye end of the body as shown.
7 Wind on both hackles together at least three or four turns to improve floating. Tie off and trim unwanted hackle ends. Add a whip finish and varnish it.

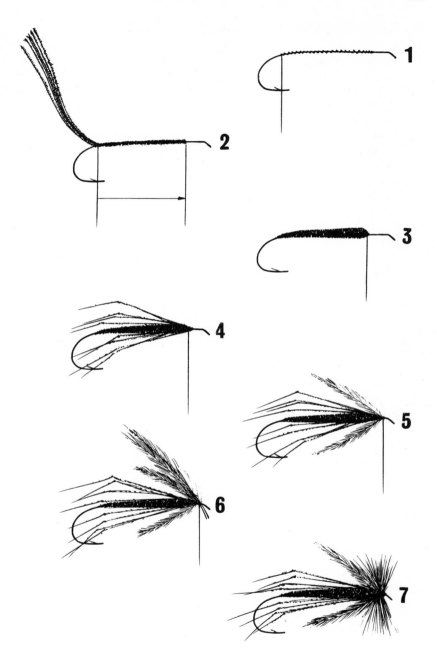

30 Gold Ribbed Hare's Ear

traditional

According to G. L. Herter, the Gold Ribbed Hare's Ear was made by a fly-tyer named David Hemming of Redditch in 1832 although he does not specifically say that it was invented by him. Whilst an old pattern, it was preceded by many other flies composed of fur from the hare's ear, but this pattern has excelled them all and is now not only known, but used, throughout the world. In addition, it is a simple fly to tie. This is a fly in which one may have absolute confidence as did many great anglers of the past, including F. M. Halford who applauded it in several of his books. In *Dry Fly Entomology* he gives an excellent description of the fly, which I quote: 'From early spring to late autumn it is the most killing of all the duns and is, besides, pre-eminently the fly to be recommended for bulging and tailing fish. It is probably taken for the sub-imago emerging from the larval envelope of the nymph just risen to the surface.' This last comment states the true position, in my opinion, thus the Gold Ribbed Hare's Ear needs to be fished either in the surface film or only just below it and, for this purpose, needs no wings. As a nymph transposing into dun, it will suffice for most of the olives provided it is tied in appropriate sizes.

Materials

Hook   Down eye, sizes 12, 14 or 16, 14 being most common
Working Silk   Primrose or light yellow
Tail   Several light coloured hairs from the edge of the hare's ear
Body   A dubbing of short dark fur not cut, but pinched with the nails, from the hare's ear to give random lengths
Legs   Longer hairs from the ear incorporated into the last two turns of body dubbing, applied at the eye end, which are then pricked out to appear as legs
Body Rib   Either fine flat gold tinsel or oval gold tinsel

Tying Operations   (refer to diagrams)

1   Wind on the working silk from a little behind the eye to the start of the bend. Cut several long hairs from the edge of the ear and tie these in to extend as shown. Follow with a short length of gold tinsel.

2   Well wax the working silk. Pinch, not cut, a little dark fur from the outside of the ear and dub this on to the silk.

3   Wind on the dubbed silk, thickening slightly towards the eye by adding a little more fur if necessary, but stop short of the eye. Before winding on the last two turns, incorporate some of the longer hairs from the ear into the dubbing.

4   Pick up the tinsel and wind this on in open turns to the eye end of the body. Tie off, trim out any surplus tinsel, wind a neat head completing with a whip finish which should be varnished.

5   Finally, using a fine-pointed dubbing needle, prick out some of the longer hairs at the eye end to represent legs.

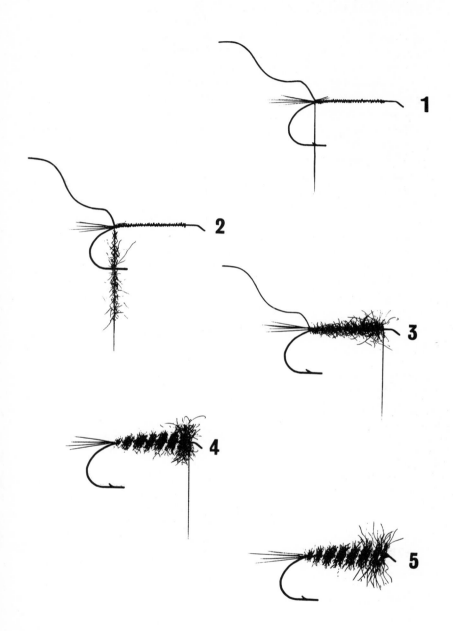

31   Grannom

Pat Russell

Occurring on many rivers mainly in the spring but somewhat later in northerly areas, this fly is of importance to anglers for it is a small *day-flying* sedge of the order *Trichoptera*, entomological name *Brachycentrus subnubilus*. When hatches occur they usually take place in the late morning when the flies can on occasion appear in dense clouds, albeit briefly, and again, but more sparsely, in the afternoon. However, I have the impression that they hatch in smaller numbers now than in the past, possibly due to the widespread use of insecticides. The trout appear to have a preference for the female who, soon after mating, carries a green egg sac at the extremity of her abdomen and it seems probable that this fly was, and still is by some people, called the Greentail Fly for this reason. This pattern, based on the female, is normally fished dry but is also effective when sunk.

Materials
Hook   Optional, up or down eye, size 14
Working Silk   Green
Tip   Green, daylight fluorescent wool
Body   Three or four natural heron herls
Wing   A bunch of blue dun cock hackle fibres
Head Hackle   Natural ginger, cock

Tying Operations   (refer to diagrams)
1   Wind on the working silk from behind the eye to the start of the bend at which point the fluorescent wool is tied in. The working silk is then wound a little towards the eye.
2   Wind on the fluorescent wool to form a short tip. Tie off and trim out excess wool. Select the heron herls and tie these in, the cut ends pointing towards the eye. Then wind the working silk to a little short of the eye covering the heron stubs as you go.
3   Varnish the shank and whilst it is still wet twist the herls into a rope and wind the rope on in tight, touching turns to where the silk hangs. Tie off and trim out the excess herl ends.

4   Select a hackle which will provide a bunch of hackle fibres slightly longer than the hook when these are torn or cut out. Place these over the shank with the fine points extending beyond the bend and tie them in securely to lie as shown. A small droplet of varnish on the securing turns will help. Then trim the hackle points off square.
5   Select and tie in the head hackle with the flat plane of the hackle at 90° to the hook shank and the outer bend facing the eye.
6   Wind on the hackle three to five turns (depending on how bushy you like your flies to appear) and leave the hackle tip clipped in hackle pliers. Then, keeping the working silk *taut,* wind this through the hackle to behind the eye, separating the fibres with a dubbing needle as you go to avoid crushing them. Secure the hackle, the tip and butt of which can then be trimmed out, wind a neat head and complete with a whip finish which should be varnished.

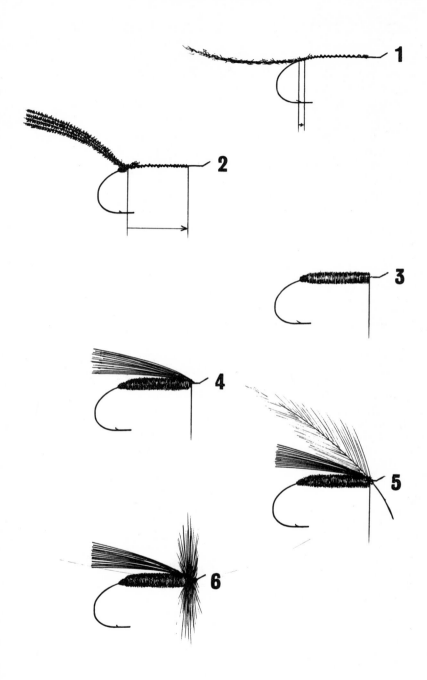

32 Greenwell – hackled variant

Whether or not Canon Greenwell would have approved of this variation on his original pattern I do not know, but it is a fact that a great many trout anglers prefer a hackled fly to one incorporating wings composed of paired slips from primary wing feathers. One view is that such wings are too opaque when compared with the gauzy wings of the natural Olive which the Greenwell is generally held to represent, whilst there are those who find the winging procedure too bothersome.

This hackled pattern has been in use for a considerable length of time and is thus tried, tested and approved. Therefore, if a hackled pattern is preferred, this is the fly for you. Trout and grayling will, may I add, like it too!

Materials

Hook Up eye, size 14 or 16; 12 occasionally useful

Working Silk Light yellow, well waxed to appear a dirty olive

Tails Four fibres from a furnace hackle

Body Built up with working silk increasing in thickness slightly towards the eye

Body Rib Optional, but when used, fine gold wire

First Hackle Cock, coch-y-bondhu or furnace as substitute

Second Hackle Cock, medium blue dun

Tying Operations (refer to diagrams)

1 Wind on the working silk from a little behind the eye to the start of the bend in close, tight, turns.

2 Tear the tail fibres from a fairly large hackle and tie these in where the silk hangs so that they point slightly down and are well spread. Follow with the gold wire.

3 Wind on the working silk back and forth building up a slightly tapered body thickening towards the eye.

4 Wind on the gold wire in six or seven tight but open turns. Tie off at the eye end of the body and trim out the surplus wire.

5 Select a hackle of each type and of a size appropriate to the size of hook used. Strip, or cut away, the lower one-third of each at the butt end and place them together, natural bends both facing the same way but with the blue dun nearest to the eye. Both hackles are then tied in at approximately 90° to the hook shank and with the outer bend of the hackles towards the eye.

6 With the tips of both hackles secured in hackle pliers, wind them on together for two to four turns according to whether you prefer a lightly or heavily hackled fly but remember that the stiffer the hackling is made the less collapsibility there will be when the fish attempts to suck it into its mouth. The hackle being wound, secure the tip with working silk ensuring that none of the fibres is trapped and forced out of place, trim out the hackle tips and butts, wind a neat head and complete with a whip finish which then varnish.

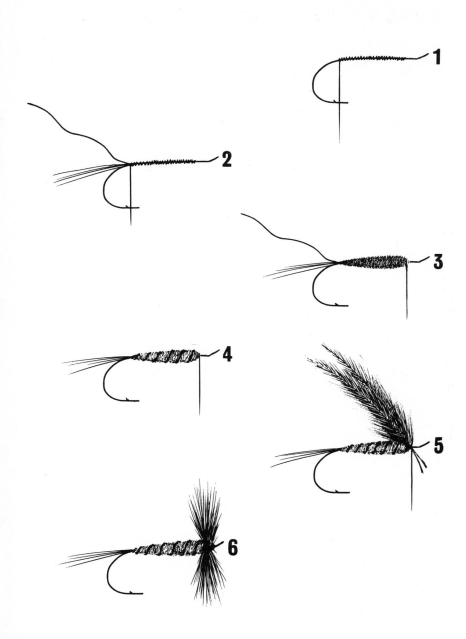

33 Grey Duster

traditional

Just as Halford described the Red Quill as 'the sheet anchor of the dry fly fisherman on a strange river,' similarly would I describe the Grey Duster and by no means to be despised for lakes and reservoirs. There have been many suggestions as to what the Grey Duster represents, but it is generally accepted as representative of the Stone Flies (*Plecoptera*), mainly February Red, Willow Fly, Small Brown. It is a good general purpose all-season dry fly which, in my experience, does best in early to mid-season. It has the advantage of being a buoyant fly and the white in the badger hackle makes it easy to see in most conditions of light, which can be a blessing. It is of value for both trout and grayling. Whisks are sometimes added to the dressing but, speaking for myself, I have found they are of little benefit other than to add to the already good floating properties of this fly.

Materials

Hook Up eye, size, 12, 14 or 16
Working Silk Brown
Body A dubbing of light rabbit or hare fur with a little blue underfur included
Hackle Badger, well-marked black centre with white edges rather than cream

Tying Operations (refer to diagrams)

1 Wind on the working silk from a little behind the eye to the start of the hook bend.
2 Well wax the working silk and dub on the body fur, not too thickly.
3 Wind on the dubbed fur, thin at the bend end of the body but thickening slightly towards the eye. When satisfied with the body, remove any excess fur from the working silk.
4 Select, prepare and tie in the hackle at the eye end of the body, the flat plane of the hackle at 90° to the fly body as in 4A, the outer bend towards the eye.

5 Using hackle pliers or fingers wind on the hackle four to six close turns, depending on the size of the hook used, ending with the hackle tip hanging in the pliers.
6 Keeping the working silk *taut,* wind it carefully through the hackle to behind the eye, ensuring that the hackle fibres are not compressed by separating them with a dubbing needle as the working silk is wound through, and that the hackle tip is secured. Remove the hackle pliers and trim out the hackle tip and butt.
Complete with a whip finish which should then be varnished.

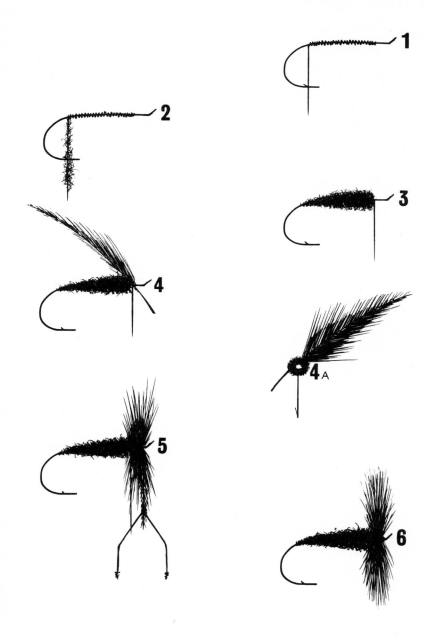

34 Grey Wulff

Lee Wulff

Although animal hair is generally considered to have been introduced into fly dressing towards the end of the last century, the use of this material really achieved wider acceptance when, in the 1930s, Lee Wulff evolved his series of flies, now so well known, which were the forerunners of many patterns incorporating hair of different kinds for tails, bodies and wings. The use of hair has, over the years, permeated into every type of fly-dressing and is now commonplace. Not all hair is suitable for all purposes and the relative usefulness of each needs to be assessed to achieve maximum advantage, therefore one must experiment. Jack Dennis (USA) expresses the view in his *Western Trout Fly Tying Manual* (1974) that the Grey Wulff is basically a hair wing Blue Dun whilst others have accepted it as a representation of the Mayfly. It matters not a scrap for under both guises it takes its fair share of fish in the USA and in the UK. In smaller sizes the superb floating qualities of this Wulff pattern will readily be apparent when used on fast moving ruffled waters. Elk hair is recommended for tail and wings but bucktail or calftail is now often used instead. The series includes White, Brown, Black and Royal Wulff.

Materials

Hook   Up or down eye, sizes 8 to 16
Working Silk   Black
Tail   Brown elk, bucktail or calftail hair
Body   Grey rabbit underfur dubbing is most common; muskrat, mole or blue-grey seal fur dubbing also used
Wings   As for tail
Hackle   Two are required: they can be light or medium blue dun or badger dyed (or photo-dyed) medium blue dun; smallish saddle hackles may be found advantageous for the larger sizes

Tying Operations   (refer to diagrams)

1 Starting at the centre of the hook shank, wind on the working silk in close turns to the start of the bend at which point a bunch of hairs is tied in so that the cut ends reach the centre of the shank and the fine points a shank length beyond the bend. Tying down the hair, wind the working silk back to the centre.
2 A second bunch of hairs is then tied in to extend over the eye and the working silk wound over them but leaving plenty of room at the eye.

3 Lift the hairs over the eye up to about 80° and take two turns round the hook shank tight up against the wing hairs to support them. Divide these hairs into two and use the figure-of-eight binding for an open 'V' position. Then wind the working silk back to the start of the bend.
4 Well wax the working silk and dub the fur on to the silk ready to wind on for the body. Then varnish the shank.
5 Wind on the dubbed fur in close turns thickening towards the wings. Any excess fur can then be removed from the working silk.
6 Select the hackles, strip off the fluffy base and tie in both together behind the wings at right angles to the shank with the outer bends facing the eye. Then bring the working silk under the shank to behind the eye.
7 Wind on both hackles two turns
7A behind and two turns in front of the wing. Tie off with working silk, trim out the hackle tip and butt, wind a neat head and complete with the whip finish which then varnish. 7A shows a front view of the finished fly.

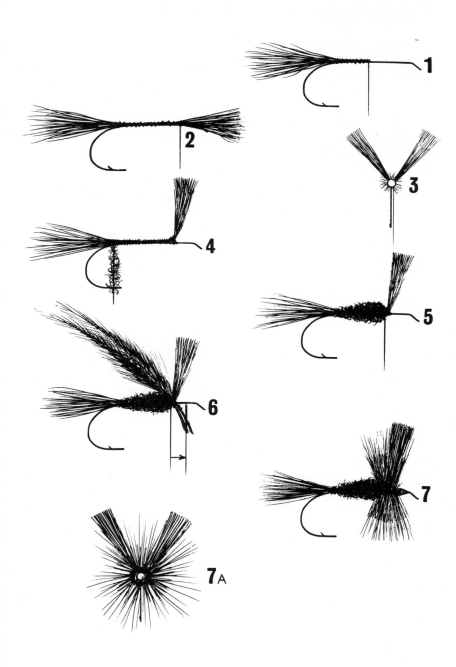

35 Hacklepoint Coachman

variation of traditional

When a man like David Collyer writes that this fly has accounted for more fish for him than perhaps any other, one has to take note. He has used it effectively on many stillwaters in England and Wales but it is in the late evening on rivers that it excels.

The hacklepoint wings, more broken in outline than the normal solid fibre wings, may tend to reflect the local colour of the water or vegetation and appear less harshly white and thus more akin to the gauzy wing of natural flies as seen by the fish. For the angler they provide the focal point on which one can concentrate and keep in touch – they will even pick up the blaze of the setting sun. One innovation Collyer has introduced is to trim off the hackle fibres below the fly so that they just exceed the gape of the hook. This allows the fly to alight in its correct upright position more often than not and, in addition, permits it to settle a little lower in the water in a natural stance.

Materials

Hook   Up eye, size 14, 12 or 10
Working Silk   Sherry spinner
Body   Three or four natural bronze peacock herls taken from the stem, not the eye
Wings   Two hacklepoints from white cock hackles
Hackle   Natural ginger or red game, cock

Tying Operations   (refer to diagrams)

1   Wind on the working silk from a little behind the eye to the start of the bend.
2   Cut the peacock herls from the stem and tie them in so that they extend beyond the bend. Then wind the working silk back over two-thirds of the shank.
3   Varnish the turns of silk on the shank and whilst still wet wind on the peacock herls, either in a bunch or twisted into a rope, until the working silk is reached. Tie off and trim out any surplus herl ends.
4   Select the two white cock hackles for the wings and lay them together so that the better (shiny) sides face each other and trim off the base leaving hackle points slightly longer than the body of the fly. These are then tied in together, wet fly style, so that they lie over the body as shown.

5   Grasp the hacklepoint wings firmly and, lifting them to the vertical, manipulate two turns of working silk tightly up behind and against the base of the wings to keep them in that position. Next, separate the wings and secure them in an open 'V' position with a figure-of-eight binding, i.e., take the working silk between the wings, round the shank in front of the wings, back diagonally between the wings and once more round the shank behind the wings.
6   Two, possibly three such bindings may be needed to ensure the correct winging position shown in diagram 6.
7   Select the hackle and tie this in on the eye side of the wings at right angles to the shank, the outer bend facing the eye.
8   Wind on two turns in front of the wings, then one turn diagonally through the wings and two turns behind. Take the silk under the hook and secure the hackle tip behind the wings. Trim out the hackle tip then, keeping it taut, wind the silk back through the hackle to behind the eye ensuring that the fibres are not caught and spoiled in shape. Wind a neat head completing with a whip finish which should be varnished.
9   This shows a front view of the finished fly.

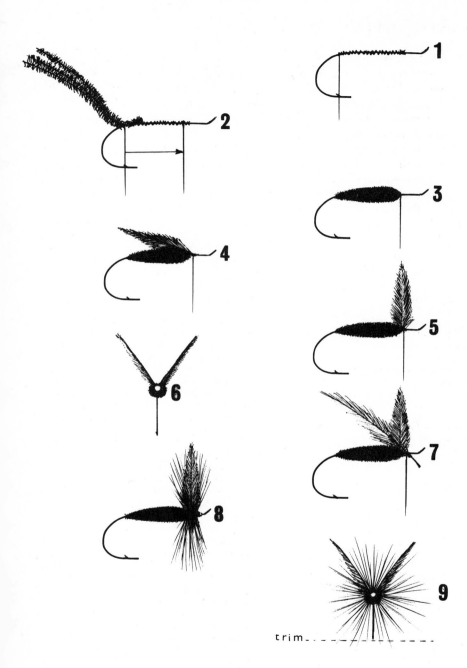

36 Imperial

Oliver Kite

The three flies I usually associate with the Large Dark Olive (*Baëtis rhodani*) are the Rough Olive, Olive Quill and, in my view the best, Kite's Imperial. His use of purple silk slightly to colour the natural heron herl is surely one of the reasons for its success and the acclaim which this fly has justly received since its invention in the 1960s.

The Large Dark Olive is prevalent on many and varied waters from placid streams to peaty, tumbling, rocky rivers during the early season (March/April) and late autumn. The Imperial, a dry fly, is excellent for trout and, at the season end, for grayling.

Materials

Hook   Up or down eye, size 14 in spring; 15 or 16 later
Working Silk   Purple
Tail   March and April grey/brown, honey dun later
Body   Three natural undyed heron herls from a primary wing feather
Body Rib   Fine gold wire
Thorax Hump   Ends of heron herl doubled and redoubled
Hackle   Honey dun cock; very pale ginger cock as substitute

Tying Operations   (refer to diagrams)

1   Wind on the working silk ⅛ in. (3 mm.) from behind the eye to the start of the bend.
2   Tie in the tails, gold wire and heron herls in that order. Then wind the working silk back over two-thirds of the hook shank.
3   Varnish the shank and whilst it is still wet wind on the heron herls clockwise to the hook shank until the working silk is reached. *Do not* trim herl ends.
4   Wind on the gold wire in open turns anti-clockwise to the hook shank until the working silk is reached. Tie off; trim surplus wire. Then wind the working silk back over a quarter of the hook shank by one open turn. Pull the heron herl ends to the rear over the body and tie down forming the first layer of the thorax. Again, *do not* trim herl ends. Then wind the working silk forward to behind the eye by one open turn.
5   Pull the heron herl ends forward and down to the eye and tie down. Trim any ends remaining.
6   The thorax is now complete and the fly should appear thus.
7   Select and tie in the cock hackle with the flat plane at right angles to the shank, the outer bend facing the eye.
8   Wind the silk slightly towards the eye. The hackle is then wound on in close turns and secured behind the eye.
9   Tie off and complete with a whip finish which should be varnished.

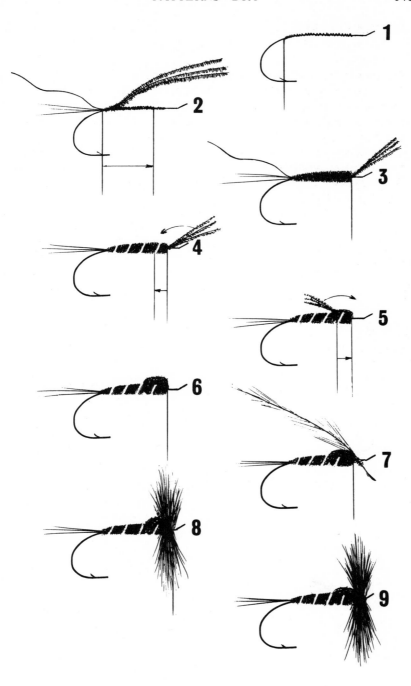

37   Iron Blue Dun

Freddie Rice

The Iron Blue Dun, *Baëtis pumulis* or *B. niger* is, once recognised, a fairly easy fly to identify being small with a short, dark, thick-set body, two tails and four wings of dark slate-blue colour. Widely distributed, except in south-east England, it is found on large and small rivers, both placid and fast flowing, and on pebbly streams. Hatches, though most prolific in May and June, can occur intermittently throughout the season and sometimes in surprising numbers when least expected on days of cold, squally showers. Bear in mind that late season flies can be small and light in colour. The Iron Blue has long been known as a fly of which the trout are very fond and over the last 200 years or so many patterns have evolved. Some have incorporated silk or other material of claret, a colour not found in the dun but these were, perhaps, intended as dual purpose dun-cum-spinner flies, the claret included for the female spinner, the Little Claret, the body and thorax of which is claret tinged. The colouring below is close to the male as given by John Goddard, *Trout Fly Recognition*.

Materials

Hook   Up eye, size 16
Working Silk   Olive
Tails   Two medium-to-dark olive hackle fibres; see note below
Body   Herls from a dark slate-grey heron primary; these can be dyed or dipped in picric acid to impart an olive tint as in the natural
Wings   Paired slips taken from starling primary feathers dyed slate-blue
Hackle   Dark olive-brown, cock

Tying Operations   (refer to diagrams)

1   Wind on the working silk from a little behind the eye to the start of the bend.
2   Tie in the tail fibres to project slightly downward followed by the heron herls for the body. Then wind the working silk back and forth to a little behind the eye forming a tapered underbody as you go.
3   Varnish the turns of silk on the shank and whilst it is still wet wind on the heron herls to where the silk hangs. Trim out the herl ends.
4   Cut a slip from each of a left and a right starling wing primary and, placing them back to back, tie them in to lie over the shank, wet fly tyle. Varnish the joint.

5A   Grasp the wings firmly and, lifting
5B   them to the vertical, take two or three turns of silk round the shank behind and hard up against the wing bases to support them. Using a dubbing needle, separate the wing slips into an open 'V' and use figure-of-eight turns of silk to secure them as at 5B, the silk to end up on the bend side of the wings.
6   Select and tie in the hackle behind the wings at right angles to the shank and with the outer bend towards the eye. Then take the working silk under the shank to the eye side of the wings.
7   Wind on the hackle two turns behind the wings thus adding more support to them and then in between the wings to the front of the wings where two more turns should be wound on. The hackle tip is then secured with working silk.
8   Trim out the hackle tip and butt, wind a neat head and complete with a whip finish which should be varnished.

Note   Taut fibres are easily lost in use, so dressings frequently specify four or more, even though the natural fly may have only two. If several are used, splay them out and set with silk or varnish to aid the fly's floating capability.

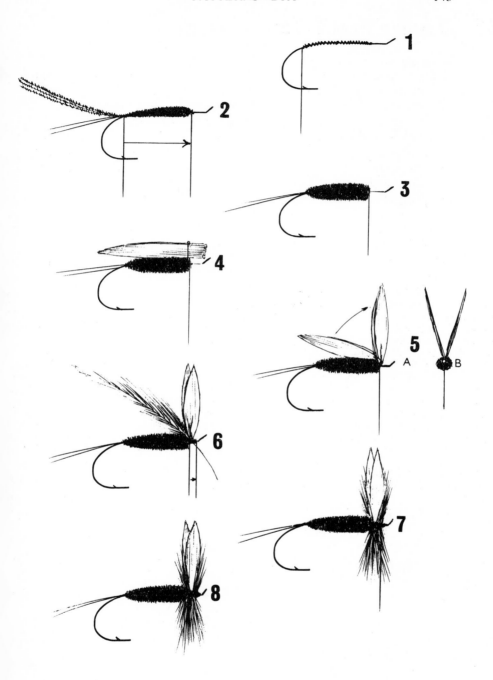

38 Large Dark Olive Dun

Freddie Rice

There can be little doubt that the Large Dark Olive (*Baëtis rhodani*) is a hardy fly, for it sometimes appears as early as February in congenial weather and when the season opens may well be found to be the only dun on the water. As we move into April hatches increase but are virtually over by early summer, although insubstantial hatches may still appear intermittently. It is not really until the season is about to close that it makes its reappearance, to the joy of the grayling fisher. It is probably one of our most common and widespread upwinged flies and can be found on many waters including big, fast-flowing rivers, placid streams and small, bubbling brooks.

Materials

Hook   Up eye, size 14
Working Silk   Olive
Tails   Four fibres of body length from a light blue dun hackle.
Underbody   Working silk built up slightly towards the eye
Overbody   White moose mane hairs dyed dark browny-olive or dark greeny-olive but lighter in late spring and in autumn
Wings   Paired slips of pale starling primary feathers
Hackle   Medium olive, cock

Tying Operations   (refer to diagrams)

1   Wind on the working silk from a little short of the eye to the start of the hook bend at which point the four tail fibres are tied in. Then, using the thumb nail, press them against the shank to spread them a little. Set with varnish.
2   Tie in the moose mane hairs near, but not at, the fine tips, then wind on the working silk back and forth to form a thin tapered body. Leave the silk at the eye end.
3   Wind on the two moose mane hairs together without allowing them to twist until the end of the underbody is reached. Tie off and remove any surplus hair.
4   Cut matching slips approximately ³/₁₆ in. (5 mm.) wide from left and right primary feathers, place them back to back, dark sides outward and tie them in to lie over the body.

5   Grip the wings firmly and lift them so that they are almost upright. With the other hand manipulate two turns of working silk round the shank and *tightly* up behind the wings to support them. Use the dubbing needle to separate the wings and apply a figure-of-eight binding to keep them in an open 'V' position.
6   Strip the fluffy fibres from the base of the hackle and tie the hackle in behind the wings with the outer bend facing the eye.
7A   Wind on the hackle two tight turns
7B   hard up against the wings, then go diagonally through the wings and take two final turns in front of the wings. Tie off, trim out the hackle butt and tip, wind a neat head completing with the normal whip finish which then varnish.

Note   The natural fly has two tails but one tends to lose the odd fibre in use and also four fibres add to the floating capabilities of the fly.

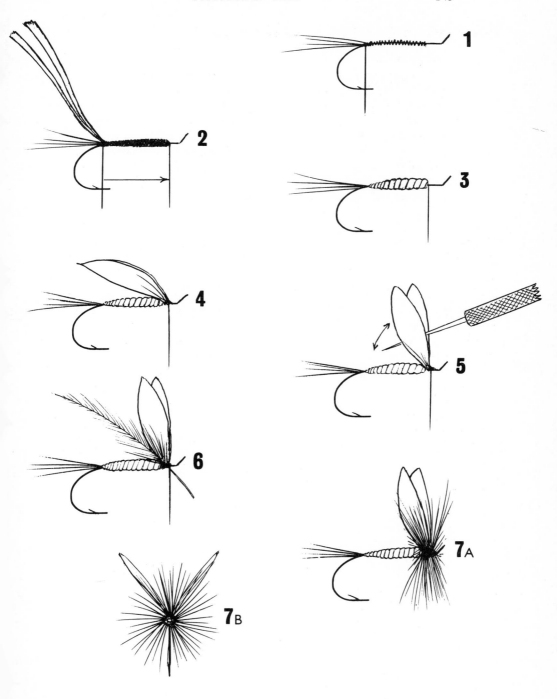

39 Last Hope

John Goddard

Originally produced to represent the Pale Watery Dun it was in practice found to be extremely effective when any small flies were on the water. John stresses the need to use a very small hook and a hackle that has a very short flue – somewhat difficult to come by. Whilst clipping the fibres of a normal small hackle is generally considered anathema to any know-ledgeable fly-tyer, it may be necessary as the only alternative for this fly. For early season work he recommends the lighter bodied buff pattern and from mid-June onwards the darker grey pattern. It may be a tiny fly but it has accounted for a large number of big trout.

Materials

Hook   Up eye, size 17 or 18
Working Silk   Pale yellow
Tail Whisks   Six to eight honey dun cock hackle fibres
Body   Two or three Norwegian goose herls, preferably from a breast feather, or condor herls, light buff in colour for early season or dark grey mid-June onwards
Hackle   Small, sharp cream cock having very short fibres

Tying Operations   (refer to diagrams)

1   Wind on the working silk in close turns from a little behind the eye to the start of the bend.
2   Strip the fibres for the tail from a fairly large hackle. These are then tied in so that they extend well beyond the bend as shown followed by the body herls. Then wind the working silk back to a little short of the eye.
3   Varnish the hook shank and whilst it is still wet wind on the body herls in close turns to just short of the eye. Tie off and trim out surplus herl ends.
4A   Select and tie in the hackle at the
4B   eye end of the body as shown. Then wind the working silk to just behind the eye.
5   Wind on the hackle two to four turns close together. Tie off with working silk and trim out the remaining hackle tip and butt. Add a whip finish and varnish the whip. Avoid daubing the hackle with varnish.

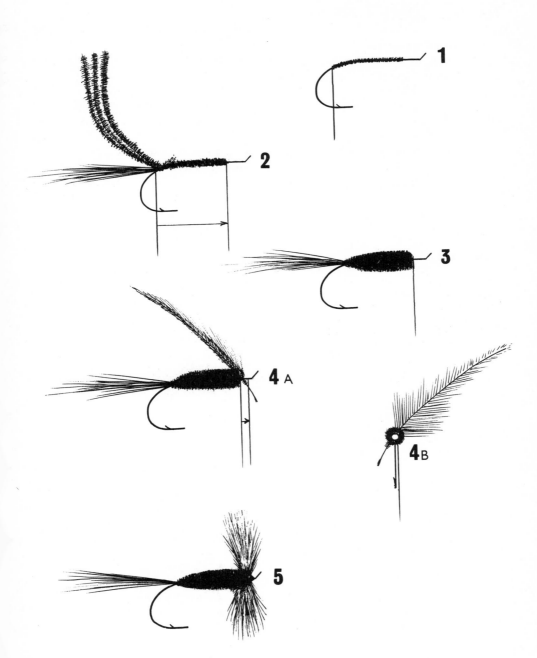

40 Light Cahill

Daniel Cahill

This is an old favourite in eastern states of the USA, still highly regarded as a general pattern dry fly and, since it is also suggestive of a number of Ephemeroptera, will suffice for *Stenonema ithaca* and *Siphlonurus quebecensis,* amongst others. It was invented in 1880 by an Irishman of Port Jervis, New York, a brakeman on the Erie Railroad. Two points are worthy of comment. The first concerns the material used for the wings which was originally taken from wood duck flank feathers, now in short supply. An acceptable substitute will be found in flank feathers from the mallard drake. The second concerns the angle at which the wings are set when the fly is viewed sideways on. Some people prefer the tips of the wings to lean forward over the eye of the hook at an angle of about 80°. I suggest you try both, leaving the selection to the trout!

Materials

Hook   Up or down eye, size 10, 12 or 14

Working Silk   Grey or ash

Wings   A bunch of fibres from a wood duck or mallard drake flank feather

Tails   Fibres from a wood duck breast feather or mallard drake flank feather

Body   Creamy-white seal fur or pale creamy-grey wool

Hackle   Grey-buff, buff or ginger, cock

Tying Operations   (refer to diagrams)

1 Wind on a few turns of working silk from a little behind the eye and towards the bend. Tear out an adequate bunch of fibres from the flank feather and tie it in horizontally over the shank with the fine points extending over the eye as shown. Varnish the securing turns then continue winding the working silk to the start of the bend where the tails are then tied in.

2 Well wax the silk and dub on a little seal fur.

3 Wind on the dubbed fur forming the body which needs to be thickened towards the eye as it covers the butt ends of the wing fibres.

4 The working silk, having been cleaned of any surplus fur, is wound a few turns towards the eye and varnished.

5A Grasp the wing fibres firmly and lift
5B them to the vertical or, if you prefer, to an angle of 80° above the eye. Manipulate several turns round the base of the wing fibres and either separate them into two equal bunches with a dubbing needle and secure them in an open 'V' position with figure-of-eight turns of silk as in 5B, or the fibres can be left as a single undivided wing. The working silk should end up on the bend side of the wings.

6 Select the hackle and tie this in behind the wings at right angles to the shank with the outer bend facing the eye. Then take the silk under the shank to the front of the wings.

7A Wind on the hackle two turns bend
7B side of the wings then under the shank to the eye side of the wings and do two more turns. Tie off, trim out the hackle butt and tip, wind a neat head, do a securing whip finish and then varnish.

Note   For the Dark Cahill, change the body to muskrat or any fine brown fur, adding a gold tip, and the hackle to brown or medium red game. It is the better fly for British waters and is an adequate representation of *Siphlonurus lacustris,* the large summer dun, found in the north and west.

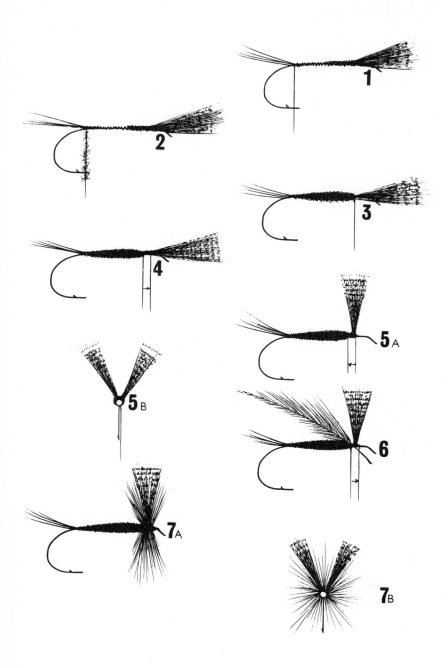

41   Little Dorrit

Freddie Rice

I like this pattern for two reasons. Firstly, because the white wing helps me to keep in touch in times of dull and overcast skies and, secondly, having no hackle points below the hook, the fly sits *in* the surface film. It was originally tied for the Pale Watery but it has developed into a very useful pattern well worth trying whenever a pale coloured fly is on the water which, at a distance, defies specific recognition.

Flies tied in the 'Parachute' style, originally developed by Alexander Martin of Glasgow and patented by him in 1933, consistently land hook down and in such a gentle manner that the most wary of fish is unlikely to be frightened off. As will be seen, the hackle is wound horizontally round the base of the wing which allows the fly to sit on, rather than be suspended by the legs above, the surface. Where split hair wings are used, two hackles, one wound 'Parachute' style round each of the wing bases, will give you the 'Waterwalker' style introduced by Frank Johnson of Streamside Anglers, Missoula, Montana, USA.

Materials

Hook   Up eye, size 12, 14 or 16; 14 the most common
Working Silk   Pale straw or primrose
Tails   Several fibres from a cream cock hackle
Body   Natural cream fine seal fur
Wing   A small bunch of white calftail fibres
Hackle   Cream, cock, tied 'Parachute' style round the wing root

Tying Operations   (refer to diagrams)

1   Wind on a few turns of working silk a little behind the eye. Cut a small bunch of calftail fibres for the wing and level up the tips a little. Tie in these fibres so that the fine tips overhang the eye as shown. Then wind the working silk down the shank to the start of the bend covering the fibres as you go. Then tie in the hackle fibres for the tail.
2   Well wax the working silk and dub on the seal fur ready for winding.
3   Varnish the shank, including the covered ends of the wing, then wind on the seal fur dubbing, thinly at first but thickening later, forming the body. Strip off any dubbing remaining on the silk and wind it slightly towards the eye.

4   Varnish the turns of silk on the eye side of the body.
5   Lift the wing fibres to the vertical and take several turns of silk round them as near to the shank as possible, then two turns round the shank but hard up against the wing on the eye side to give added support. The working silk is then wound to the bend side of the wing.
6   Select and tie in the hackle on the bend side of the wing at right angles to the shank but with the flat plane lying along the shank ready to be wound horizontally round the wing base. That done, wind the silk to the eye side of the wing.
7   With the hackle tip in pliers wind the hackle horizontally round the base of the wing post keeping the turns close together. When three or four turns are wound on, pull the hackle tip along the shank to the eye. Secure the hackle tip with working silk after pulling the wing post towards the bend which will lift the horizontal hackle fibres away from the eye. Trim hackle tip and butt. Wind a neat head, complete with a whip finish which should be varnished.

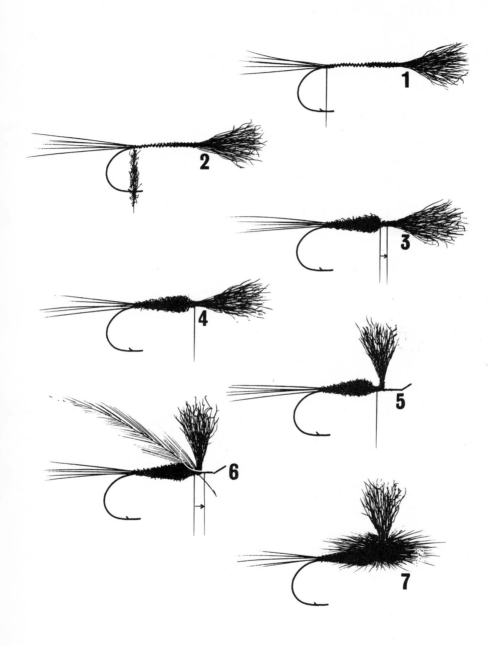

42 Orange Quill

G. E. M. Skues

It was G. E. M. Skues who discovered this pattern although he did not invent it. He copied a pattern he found in a tackle-dealer's shop in Winchester which met his requirements for a larger than normal fly. By all accounts he quickly found it to be an ideal imitation of the Blue Winged Olive, suitable for both trout and grayling. Whether it is taken as the dun or the spinner is debatable, but it is a reliable fly to have to hand from June on when the Blue Winged Olive is on the water, particularly when the natural is hatching at dusk. The original body material was pale condor quill, stripped, but this is no longer obtainable by most of us since the condor, a very large bird of the Andes, is now very rare. I have, therefore, substituted moose mane hairs dyed hot orange, as was the original condor quill.

Materials

Hook   Up eye, size 12 or 14
Working Silk   Hot orange
Tails   Several fibres from a natural red game or ginger hackle
Body   Two white moose mane fibres dyed hot orange
Wings   Pale starling
Hackle   Red game, cock

Tying Operations   (refer to diagrams)
1   Wind on the working silk from a little behind the eye to the start of the bend at which point tie in the tail fibres followed by the moose mane hairs set in near, but not at, their fine tips. Then wind the working silk back to where you began, forming a slim underbody.
2   Wind on both moose main hairs together in close, even turns (ensuring that they do not twist together whilst doing so), leaving enough room for wings and hackle to be tied in behind the eye. Tie off and trim out surplus ends of hair.
3   Cut a pair of slips from matched starling primary wing feathers and, placing them back to back, light sides outward, tie them in to lie as shown. Trim any excess wing stumps over the eye, then secure the joint with varnish.

4A   Grasp the wings firmly right down to
4B   where they join the hook shank and, lifting them to the vertical, take a couple of turns of working silk round the shank behind and hard up against the base of the wings to support them, followed by two turns on the eye side. Separate the wings with a dubbing needle and, using figure-of-eight turns, secure them in an open 'V' position as in 4B, the working silk to end behind the wings.
5   Select the hackle and tie this in behind the wings at right angles to the shank with the outer bend facing the eye. Then take the silk under the shank and take one turn on the eye side.
6   Wind on the hackle two turns behind the wings, which will give them additional support, and then two turns in front of them. Tie off, trim out hackle butt and tip, wind a neat head completing with the usual whip finish which should then be varnished.

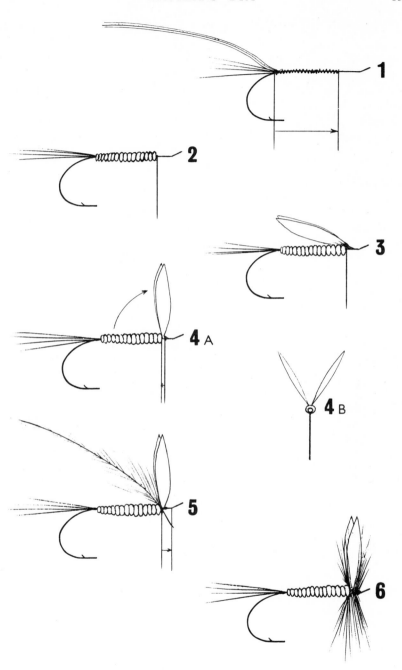

43 Pale Watery Dun

Freddie Rice

The name Pale Watery has for long been applied by anglers to several small duns of similar appearance, the difference, from one fly to another, being hardly perceptible at a cursory glance. Hence it is confused with medium and small olives. Latterly the species covered by the name have being separately defined as *Centroptilum* and *Baëtis* although it is questionable whether anything has been gained from the angler's point of view.

We are concerned with imitating a fly generally smaller than the olives and the dressing here described is based on *Baëtis bioculatus,* male, which appears mainly in May though possibly a little later in the north, and continues on through the season. It is confined principally to England and south Wales.

This is a general representative pattern which will be found useful where precise identification is difficult though assessed as of a pale and indistinct 'watery' colour. If a winged fly is prefered slips from left and right light starling primary wing feathers can be incorporated into the dressing between operations 5 and 6.

Materials

Hook   Up eye, size 14 or 16
Working Silk   Light yellow
Tails   Four light blue dun or pale honey dun hackle fibres
Tag   Four or five close turns of working silk
Underbody   Working silk
Body   Two or three herls from a light grey heron, white swan or goose wing feather dyed palest olive or steeped in picric acid for about two hours
Hackle   Palest olive or pale honey dun, cock

Tying Operations   (refer to diagrams)

1   Wind on the working silk in close turns from a little behind the eye to the start of the bend at which point the tail fibres are tied in and slightly spread with the thumb nail.
2   Using the working silk, preferably unwaxed, imitate the last body segment by winding on a tag of four close turns of silk.
3   Immediately up against the tag tie in the body fibres so that they extend over the tails.
4   Wind on the working silk forming a slim, tapered underbody finishing a little short of the eye.
5   Varnish the tapered underbody and whilst it is still wet wind on the body fibres in close turns to the eye end of the underbody. Tie off and trim out any surplus herl ends.
6   Select a good quality hackle and tie this in by the butt at right angles to the shank with the outer bend facing the eye.
7   Wind on the hackle three to five turns depending on hook size. Tie off, trim out the hackle butt and tip, wind a neat head completing with a whip finish which then varnish.

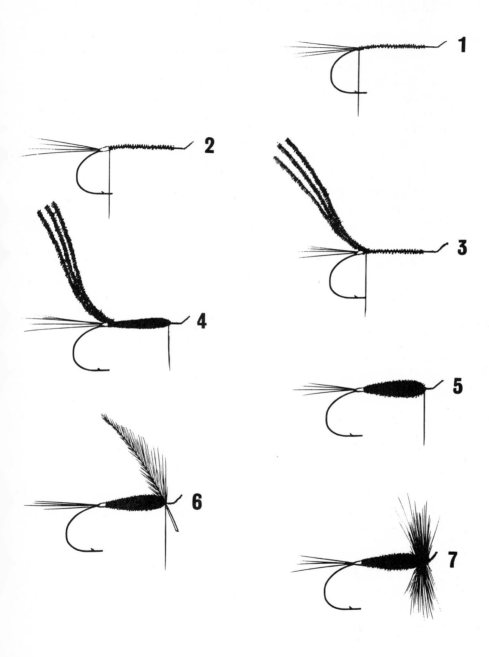

44 Quill Gordon

Theodore Gordon

Theodore Gordon was an American fly-tyer well known in the 1890s for a number of patterns he evolved. It is said that he would not divulge his fly-tying expertise to anyone although many sought his guidance, among them Reuben Cross who later found fame as a fly-tyer nevertheless. The precise dressing was never confirmed by Gordon since he apparently changed the dressing to match the hatch of the moment, thus it appears in various guises. In some cases fine gold wire is shown as a ribbing to protect the quill body; in others the hackle and tail are very pale blue, possibly light blue dun. The Quill Gordon, or Gordon Quill as it is sometimes called, has enjoyed a long period of popularity, at its peak in the 1930s, but a good standby pattern worth a try on any trout water. My own experience has been that it does best in the smaller sizes.

Materials

Hook Up or down eye, size 12 or 14
Working Silk Ash or grey
Tails Fibres from a wood duck flank feather, a blue/grey hackle or light elk hair
Body Peacock quill, stripped of flue, natural or dyed yellow or blue
Body Rib When used, fine gold wire
Wings Fibres from a wood duck flank feather or yellow dyed mallard flank feather
Hackle Light, medium or dark grey or grey with a blue tint

Tying Operations (refer to diagrams)

1 Wind on the working silk from a little behind the eye to the start of the bend in close, tight turns. At the bend, tie in the tail fibres, the stripped quill and the gold wire if being used. Then wind the working silk back to just short of the original starting point, keeping the body smooth. This is important, for bumps or depressions in the underbody prevent the quill from lying flat.
2 Wind on the stripped quill clockwise to the shank in touching turns; tie off when the working silk is reached and trim out the surplus quill.
3 Pick up the wire and wind this on anti-clockwise to the shank in open turns to where the silk hangs. Tie off and trim out the surplus wire.

4 Select a good bunch of fibres from the wood duck or mallard feather, even up the tips, and tie these in behind the eye to lie as shown. Add a touch of varnish to the securing turns and then trim out the excess fibre ends over the eye.
5 Grasp the wings and lift them to the vertical. Pass the working silk twice round the very base of the wings then wind two turns of working silk round the hook shank hard up against the wings (on the bend side) to keep them upright (see Note below). Select the hackle and tie this in on the bend side of the wings at 90° to the shank and with the outer bend facing the eye. The working silk is then taken under the shank to the eye side of the wings.
6A Clip the hackle tip in pliers and
6B wind on two turns hard up against the wing on the bend side, then two turns on the eye side. Tie off, trim out the hackle tip and butt, wind a neat head, whip finish and varnish.

Note If a divided wing is preferred, the wing when secured in operation 5 should be divided into two equal portions, opened into a 'V' shape and secured in that position using a figure-of-eight binding. See diagram 7. The hackle is wound two turns behind the wings, then once between the wings and finally two turns on the eye side.

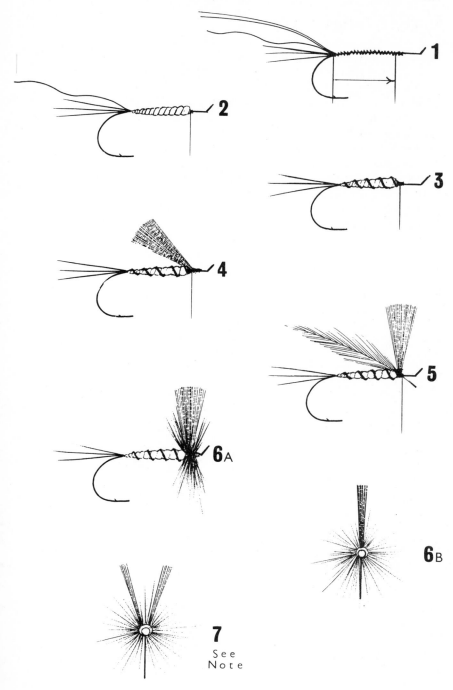

1

2

3

4

5

6A

6B

7
See
Note

45 Red Quill

attributed to Thomas Rushworth, 1803

The entomological view is that this fly represents the Claret Dun (*Leptophlebia vespertina*). However, I feel that it is more akin to a number of spinners, particularly the Sherry Spinner (*Ephemerella ignita*). Whatever the intention of the inventor, this fly is acknowledged as a good standby at any time when duns and spinners are on the water. This is, no doubt, what prompted Halford to describe the fly as 'one of the sheet anchors of the dry fly fisherman on a strange river, when in doubt.'

One of the difficulties of the dressing is that some herls recommended for stripping, which are taken from near the eye portion of the feather, do not provide a dark quill with a light edge which, when wound on, gives the appearance of a segmented body. An alternative is to use moose mane hair, one light and one dark coloured, wound on together. The light coloured hair can be dyed red (as can the peacock quill), hot orange or olive and thus one can ring the changes in body colour to suggest several flies.

Materials

Hook Up eye, size 14, 16, occasionally 12

Working Silk Brown

Tail Several natural red game hackle fibres (cock)

Body By tradition, peacock herl, stripped of its flue, best taken from near the eye, to give light and dark edges

Hackle Natural red game, cock

Tying Operations (refer to diagrams)

1 Wind on the working silk from well behind the eye to just beyond the start of the hook bend, at which point the tail fibres pointing slightly down are tied in, followed by the stripped peacock herl or moose mane fibres.

2 Wind the working silk back and forth to behind the eye, building up a slightly tapering underbody. Varnish these turns of silk.

3 Whilst the varnish is still wet, wind on the stripped peacock herl or moose mane fibres in close turns to where the silk hangs. Tie off and trim out the surplus.

4 Now tie in a single good quality red game hackle, the flat plane at 90° to the shank and the outer bend facing the hook eye.

5 Leaving the working silk at the end of the body, wind on the hackle in close, tight turns towards the eye and leave the tip hanging in the hackle pliers. Then wind the working silk, kept taut, through the hackle to the eye side. Tie off, trim out the surplus hackle tip and butt, whip finish and varnish the whip.

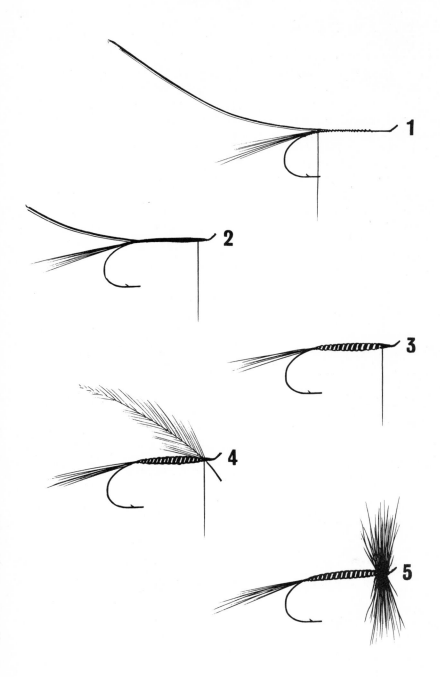

46 Sherry Spinner

Freddie Rice

This is the spinner of the female Blue Winged Olive and is well known to anglers being easily identified and common in most parts of the country. Probably the most frequently seen body shade is the colour of medium sweet sherry from which the name derives, but it can vary from a browny-olive through shades of sherry to an almost deep pinkish-red and the benefit of the light coloured moose mane hairs with which the body of this pattern is made is that it can easily be dyed almost any shade.

The Sherry Spinner generally makes its appearance in mid-June and continues to show through the middle season when hatches are more likely to occur in the evening, to the back end when it may appear from early afternoon through to late evening. On rivers, well-aerated stretches below broken water are likely to prove the most productive.

Materials
Hook Up eye, size 14
Working Silk Light yellow
Tails Either natural buff barred cree fibres, cock or the same dyed a light olive
Tag Light yellow rayon floss
Body One dark and one light moose mane hair, the light dyed browny-olive or shades of sherry through to pinkish-red
Hackle for Wings Pale ginger, cock
Head Hackle Natural light red game, cock

Tying Operations (refer to diagrams)
1 Wind on the working silk in close turns from a little behind the eye to the start of the bend at which point tie in the tail fibres followed by a short length of rayon floss. Then wind the working silk just a little towards the eye.
2 Wind on the rayon floss to form a short tag. Tie off and trim out surplus floss.
3 Select one naturally dark brown moose mane hair and one dyed as described earlier, and tie these in by their points so that they butt up close to the tag.
4 Wind the working silk back to just behind the eye forming a slightly tapered underbody as you go.

5 Wind on the two moose mane hairs together (without letting them twist round one another) to form a body with an even segmented appearance. Tie off when the underbody is covered and trim out surplus ends of moose mane.
6 Select the pale ginger hackle for the wings, the lower fibres of which should be of body length, and tie this in as shown.
7A Wind on the hackle three or four
7B turns, tie off and trim out the surplus butt and tip. Then gather the fibres into two tight bunches at right angles to the body and secure them in this position with figure-of-eight bindings. 7B shows the position at this stage.
8 Select the light red game hackle and tie this in so that it is at right angles to the body with the outer bend facing the eye. Then wind the silk three turns towards the eye.
9A Wind on the hackle three to five
9B turns keeping each turn close up to the last. Tie off, trim out the surplus butt and tip and finish with a whip which should be varnished. 9B shows a front view of the finished fly.

Note To allow the fly to sit naturally on the surface some like to remove the lower fibres between the marks 'X' and 'Y.'

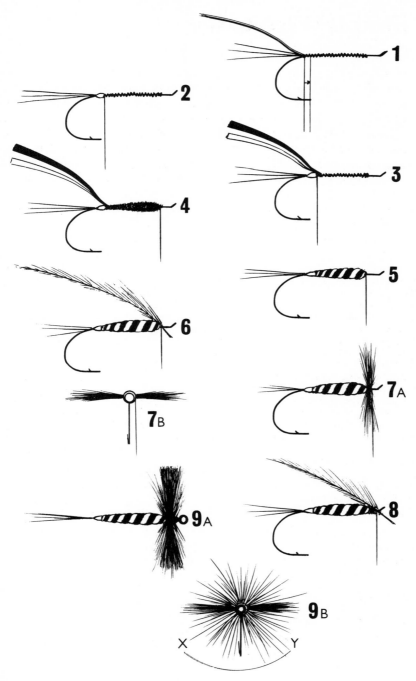

47   Simple Fredsedge

Freddie Rice

This fly is designed for simplicity and speed in tying and employs only the minimum of materials, so it is cheap to produce. It was thoroughly tested during the 1979 season and in addition to the many fish taken it also accounted for a pipistrel bat and three mallard, all at dusk, and one must assume that they took it for the real thing. None were the worse for their folly. The fly should be skated along the surface at a reasonable but even pace for the best results. If you are 'batty' enough to be willing to accept the possibility of a mixed bag when fishing, you will enjoy this fly.

Materials
Hook   Up or down eye, size 12; 10 occasionally
Silk   Brown
Body and Wings   Six to nine cock pheasant centre tail fibres, as mahogany-coloured as possible
Hackle   Two natural red game hackles

Tying Operations   (refer to diagrams)
1   Secure the silk to the shank a little behind the eye.
2   Lay the points to the bunch of pheasant tail fibres over the shank towards the bend and tie them in. Then wind the silk down the shank to the start of the bend covering the fibre points as you go. Varnish these turns of silk.
3   Whilst the varnish is still wet wind the pheasant tail fibres round the shank in close turns to where the silk hangs; they are then tied down securely, finishing with a half-hitch. The silk is then taken *over* the body to behind the eye where one turn is taken round the shank.
4   The ends of the pheasant tail fibres protruding from the bend are now drawn tightly over the body to behind the eye and tied down but the surplus is *not* trimmed off.

5   The remaining ends of these fibres which now protrude over the eye are pulled towards the rear and secured at an angle of approximately 30° by turns of silk where they join the body. The wing tips are then cut off level with the bend end of the body.
6   Two natural red game cock hackles, slightly larger than usual are then stripped at the base and tied in so that the outer bends are towards the eye.
7   Wind on these hackles three or four turns, tie off and trim out the unwanted tips remaining. Wind a neat head and add a whip finish which then varnish.

Option   As an option the two stripped butt ends of the hackles can be pulled forward and slightly upward to represent horns. They should protrude about a body length beyond the eye, as in 7A and 7B.

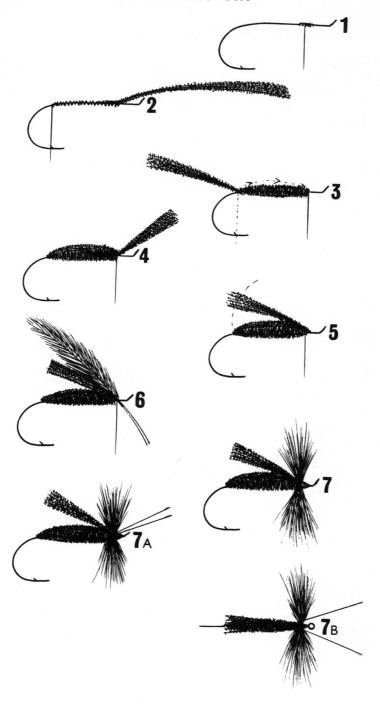

48   USD Para-Olive

Brian Clarke and John Goddard

This fly is the result of underwater observations carried out to determine what the fish sees as a fly is carried towards it on the surface of the stream.

There is no hook point or bend to show beneath the surface; the 'Parachute' form of hackle keeps the fly body lifted just clear of the stream as it is with the natural dun. The tips of the wings and the small bursts of light in the surface caused by the feet of the fly dimpling the surface provide what Clarke and Goddard believe are trigger points which may initiate a rise to the fly. The Upside Down Parachute Olive is, in consequence, a possible answer to the difficult or educated trout.

Materials

Hook   Up eye, size 12, 14 or 16
Working Silk   Orange
Tails   Two muskrat or mink whiskers or a bunch of hackle fibres coloured olive
Body   Several heron herls tinted olive by steeping in picric acid
Nylon Loop   4 lb. nylon; 'Platil Strong' is recommended
Wings   Pale blue dun hen saddle hackles
Hackle   Olive, cock

Tying Operations   (refer to diagrams)

1   Wind on the working silk from a little behind the eye to the start of the bend where the tail whiskers (or fibres) are tied in, to point slightly down, followed by the heron herls by their tips. Then wind the silk back two-thirds of the way.
2   Cut a 4 in. (10 cm.) length of nylon and tie this into protrude over the eye.
3   Form the nylon loop and tie the second joint just to the right of the first.
4   Select and tie in a hackle which should lie flat on top of the shank best side facing downward. Trim out the butt end.
5   Using wing cutters, cut a pair of wings, one wing from each hackle.
6   Turn the fly upside down in the vice. Lay the edges of the pair of wings along the shank and tie them in by the butts. Lift the wings to the vertical, take one turn hard up against the base, then separate them and secure them in an open 'V' position with a figure-of-eight binding. Trim off the butt ends.

7   Wind on the body herls to where the wings join the body. Secure them there but do not trim the surplus herl ends.
8   Turn the fly right way up in the vice, clip the hook of the gallows tool into the nylon loop and apply a little tension.
9   Grasp the end of the hackle with hackle pliers and wind it round *the base* of the nylon loop for three to five turns depending on the hook size. That done, pull the hackle tip through the nylon loop using a pair of tweezers for the purpose and, whilst keeping the tip held taut, pull the nylon loop to the right until it is *nearly* closed. Remove the gallows tool hook and pull the nylon completely to close the loop thus securing the hackle. Then apply a droplet of varnish to the nylon loop in the centre of the hackle. When it is dry, trim out the hackle tip and the surplus nylon.
10   Using hackle pliers, pick up and wind on the remainder of the heron herls to just behind the eye. Tie off, trim the surplus herl ends, whip finish and varnish with care.
11A   This shows the completed fly at this stage.
11B   Use a dubbing needle to force an outward bend to the wings, to assist the fly in settling upright on the surface.

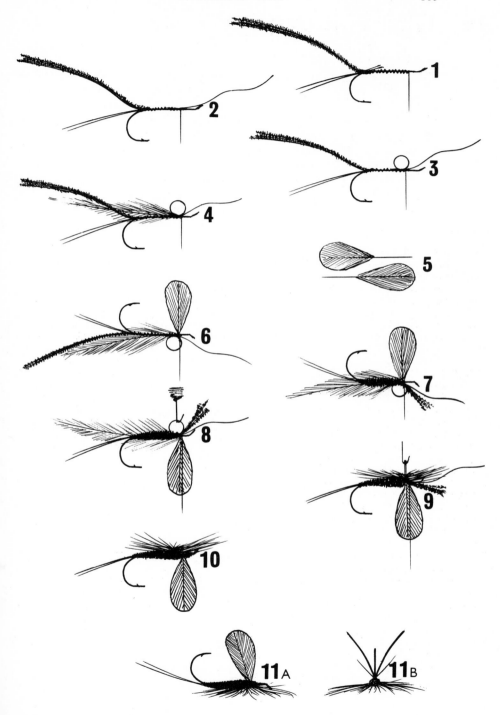

49 USD Poly-Red Spinner

Brian Clarke and John Goddard

The use of an inverted keel hook for this pattern enables the body of the fly to sit in the surface of the stream which draws the spent wings of polythene down to lie flat on the surface as do those of the natural spent spinner. The hackle, being wound 'Parachute' style, i.e., horizontally to the shank, also lies flat representing the collapsed legs of the fly. The Red Spinner is a general name loosely applied to the spinners of several up-winged duns but it would, I feel, be more appropriate to specify the spinner of the Large Dark Olive as the Large Red Spinner, that of the Medium Olive the Red Spinner and that of the Small Dark Olive the Small Red Spinner, the female being referred to in each case. Red Spinner, is thus useful during the whole season, tied in appropriate sizes.

Materials
Hook   Keel type, size 12, 14 or 16
Working Silk   Brown
Tails   Two muskrat or mink whiskers coloured pale blue are specified but three, well spread, provide balance; rabbit or hare whisker tips suffice.
Body   Red seal fur, fine not coarse
Nylon Loop   Nylon monofilament, 4 lb. breaking strain; 'Platil Strong' advocated
Hackle   Pale blue dun, cock
Wings   Very thin polythene

Tying Operations   (refer to diagrams)
1   With the hook in the vice point down, wind on the working silk in even turns to the start of the bend where the tail whiskers are tied in, then well spread and secure with a dab of varnish.
2   Turn the hook upside down in the vice. Well wax the working silk and dub a small quantity of seal fur on to the silk ready for winding on.
3   Cut about 4 in. (10 cm.) of nylon and lay one end over the shank. The dubbed seal fur is then wound on along the shank covering the nylon as you go. Remove any excess dubbing and take two turns round the shank to secure the nylon.
4   Form the nylon into a ¼ in. (6 mm.) loop and secure the loose end to the shank. Add a little dubbing to the silk and wind this on just a fraction to complete the body.

5   Select the hackle and tie this in with the flat plane of the back of the hackle uppermost, the tip then extending beyond the hook bend.
Wing Cutting   Fold a sheet of very thin polythene (*a*) in two and flatten the fold. Use wing cutters to cut the wingshape from the folded edge (*b*) so that, when it is extracted and opened it will appear as in (*c*). Hold the wings on firm cardboard and pierce them with a sharp needle.
6   Clip the hook of a gallows tool to the nylon loop and apply slight tension. With the tip of the hackle in pliers, wind the hackle round *the base* of the loop two to five turns depending on hook size. Then, using tweezers, pull the hackle tip through the loop and after clipping the pliers back on to the tip, let them hang. Pass one wing of the pair through the loop and position it as shown. Pull the loose nylon end to the right so that the loop is not quite closed. remove the hook of the gallows tool, check wing position and pull the nylon totally to close the loop which will secure the hackle and the wings in position. Trim out the hackle tip and nylon.
7A   The tricky part now.
7B   Add security to the wing centre joint by applying a figure-of-eight binding. The silk needs to be woven between the hackle fibres without destroying their positioning. Complete by winding a neat head and add a whip finish which then varnish.

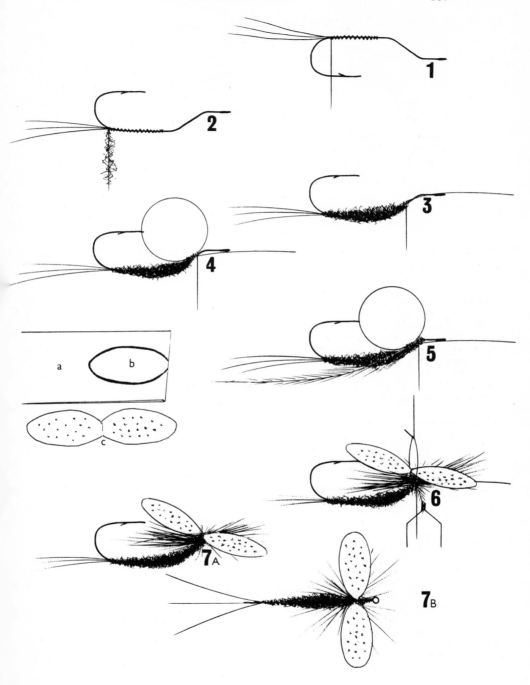

50 Walker's Sedge

Richard Walker

This fly is 'skated' across the surface at an even pace and this lifts the fly up to stand on its stiff hackles to leave a wake which, when the natural is abroad, seems particularly to stimulate the interest of the trout. The actual speed of the retrieve will either be known to you from long experience of 'sedging' or will come from trial and error. Keep the rod up and maintain the same even retrieve, resisting any impulse to speed up or slow down even if a fish is seen to be following and wait for that satisfying pull as he takes. So natural and, it seems, so attractive is the fly in this form of fly-fishing that I expect to wind down one or two mallard during the season as well as winding fish up for these birds abound where I fish and, at dusk, snatch at the fly and take off.

Materials

Hook Up or down eye, mainly 10 but 12 useful
Working Silk Brown
Tag Fluorescent orange wool
Body Eight to 12 fibres from a cock pheasant centre tail feather
Wing Either a bunch of fibres torn from a fairly long red game cock hackle or a bunch of pheasant tail fibres tied low over the body
Hackle Two red game cock hackles a little longer in the fibre than is normally used for a dry fly

Tying Operations (refer to diagrams)
1 Wind on working silk from a little short of the eye to the start of the bend.
2 Tie in 2 in. (50 mm.) of fluorescent wool, then wind working silk a little towards the eye.
3 Wind on the wool two turns to form a short tag, secure it with working silk and trim out the surplus. Cut the pheasant fibres from the tail feather and tie in the cut ends on the eye side of the tag. Then wind your working silk to a little short of the eye covering the ends of the pheasant fibres as you go.
4 Varnish the turns of silk on the shank and, whilst it is still wet, form the body by winding on the pheasant fibres in close turns to where the silk hangs and secure them with it.

5A For a wing of pheasant fibres, bend the surplus fibre ends back and low over the body and secure them in that position with the working silk. Trim these fibres off just beyond the tag.
5B The alternative type of wing is made up of a bunch of fibres from a red game cock hackle and if these are your choice the surplus pheasant tail fibres should be trimmed out when operation 4 above is completed. The red game fibres are then stripped from a fairly large hackle and tied in close to the eye end of the body so that the points lie at a low angle over the shank.
6 Next select two springy red game cock hackles and tie these in together so that their natural inner curve is towards the hook bend.
7 Wind on both hackles together for three to five turns to ensure that the fly will sit up on the water. Secure the tips with working silk and trim out the surplus tips and butts. Complete by winding a neat head ending with a whip finish which should be varnished.

Option This shows Richard Walker's earlier dressing using two furnace hackle tips (back to back) for the wing, trimmed as shown. The tag was yellow floss.

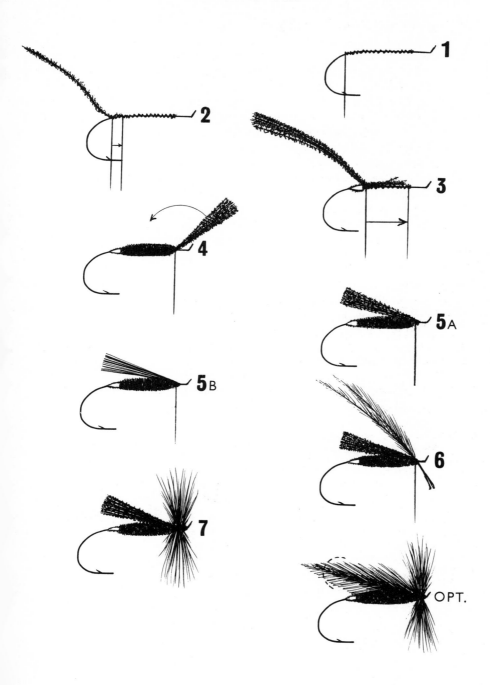

ON COLOUR

As I walked by the bank in the balmy Spring
   The Spring when the duns are out,
I marked a splash and a broadening ring,
And I hastened forward my fly to fling:
   For I knew 'twas a feeding trout –
A feeding trout; but how to entice
   Him out of his native stream?
Ah! that's the question! for once or twice
I've offered him flies which I thought as nice
In the trout's esteem, as vanilla ice
   In a lady's or strawberry cream.
Without success, for he still would feed
   On the flies which came floating past;
But of my pet lines not one would heed,
And it seemed as though it had been decreed
By some aqueous elf, that his shameful greed
Should be peacefully sated, from danger freed
   As long as the rise would last.
But at length, as the sun, at the dawn of day,
Bursts forth and chases the mists away,
Scorching the lips of the new-mown hay,
   If the clouds be not too dense;
So flashed upon me that useful hint:
"Many's the shade in a color's glint,"
A maxim straight from the coining mint,
   The mint of experience.
Then come; let us glance at this lightsome thing
With its fairy body and gossamer wing,
   "Olive encircled with yellowish rings;"
     Enough; there's the very shade.
Now craftily cast just a foot above
The nose of that *specially* wary cove –
He was the King of Trout in the *dove.*
   He rises – he's hooked – here's a game of who wins!
Even a trout's not above the pomps
   And lines of this wicked world.
In vain he gasps in unfeigned regret,
For he's safe in the folds of my landing net.

From *Ogden on Fly-tying* by James Ogden (1887)

Bibliography

BURRARD, Major Gerald, DSO, RFA (Retd), *Fly Tying: Principles & Practice,* Herbert Jenkins, 1940.

CAMERON, L. C. R. ('Sherry Spinner'), *Rod, Pole and Perch,* Martin Hopkinson, 1928.

CLARKE, Brian, and GODDARD, John, *The Trout and the Fly, A New Approach,* Ernest Benn, 1980.

COLLYER, David J., *Fly-Dressing,* David & Charles, 1975.

COURTNEY WILLIAMS, A., *Trout Flies, A Discussion and a Dictionary,* A. & C. Black, 1932.

DRAPER, Keith, *Trout Flies in New Zealand,* A. H. & A. W. Reed, 1971.

GODDARD, John, *Trout Fly Recognition,* A. & D. Black, 1966. *Trout Flies of Stillwater,* A. & C. Black, 1969.

HALFORD, F. M., *Modern Development of the Dry Fly,* George Routledge, 1910. *Floating Flies and how to Dress Them,* reprinted from first edition of 1886, Barry Shurlock, 1974.

HERTER, George Leonard, *Fly Tying, Spinning and Tackle Making,* Herter's Inc., 1971.

HILLS, Major John Waller, *River Keeper,* Geoffrey Bles, 1934.

HELLEKSON, T., *Popular Fly Patterns,* Peregrine Smith, Inc., 1976.

INGHAM, Maurice, and WALKER, Richard, *Drop me a Line,* Douglas Saunders with MacGibbon and Kee, 1953.

IVENS, Tom, *Stillwater Fly-Fishing,* Andre Deutsch, 1952.

LAWRIE, W. H., *A Reference Book of English Trout Flies,* Pelham Books, 1967. *International Trout Flies,* Frederick Muller, 1969.

LEISER, Eric, *Fly-Tying Materials,* Crown Publishers, Inc., 1973.

MARINARO, Vincent C., *A Modern Dry-Fly Code,* Crown Publishers Inc., 1950.

McCLELLAND, H. G., *How to Tie Flies for Trout,* Fishing Gazette, 1959.

MOSELEY, Martin E., *The Dry-Fly Fisherman's Entomology,* George Routledge, 1921.

OGDEN, James, *Ogden on Fly Tying,* James Ogden, Cheltenham, 1887.

RICE, Freddie, *Fly-Tying Illustrated for Nymphs and Lures,* David & Charles, 1976.
SAWYER, Frank, *Keeper of the Stream,* A. & C. Black, 1952. *Nymphs and the Trout,* A. & C. Black, 1958.
SKUES, G. E. M., *Minor Tactics of the Chalk Stream,* A. & C. Black, 1910. *The Way of a Trout with a Fly,* A. & C. Black, 1967. *Silk, Fur and Feather,* Fishing Gazette, 1950.
TAVERNER, Eric, *Trout Fishing from all Angles,* The Lonsdale Library, Seeley, Service, 1933.
VENIARD, John, *Fly Dressers' Guide,* A. & C. Black, 1952.
WALTON, Izaak, *The Compleat Angler,* Bell & Daldy, 1863.
WEST, Leonard, *The Natural Trout Fly and its Imitation,* Leonard West, St. Helens, 1912.
WOOLLEY, Roger, *Modern Trout Fly Dressing,* Fishing Gazette, Beckenham, 1932.

Other Books of Interest

HARRIS, J. R., *An Angler's Entomology,* Collins, 1952.
HENN, T. R., *Practical Fly-Tying,* A. & C. Black, 1950.
PRICE, Taff, *Stillwater Flies,* A. & C. Black, 1979.
RONALDS, Alfred, *The Fly Fisher's Entomology,* London, 1836.
SWISHER, Doug, and RICHARDS, Carl, *Selective Trout,* Crown Publishers Inc., 1971.
VENIARD, John, *Fly-Dressing Materials,* A. & C. Black, 1977. *Reservoir & Lake Flies,* A. & C. Black, 1970.
WHITLOCK, Dave, and BOYLE, Robert, Eds. *Fly Tyer's Almanac,* Crown Publishers Inc., 1975.

Index

A Booke of Fishing with Hooke and Line, 9
A Further Guide to Fly-Dressing, 23
A History of Fly-fishing for Trout, 9
A List of Natural Flies, 17
A Modern Dry Fly Code, 26, 27
A Quaint Treatise on Flees, and the Art a Artyfichall Flee Making, 17
A Reference Book of English Trout Flies, 25
Aelian (Claudius Aelianus), 7
Aldam, W. H., 17
Alder Fly, 8
Alexandra, 46, 70, 71
Athenian (McClelland, Harry), 19
All Fur Flies and How to Dress Them, 25
Appetiser, 46
Austin, R. S., 23

Baëtis bioculatus, 154
Baëtis niger, 108, 142
Baëtis pumilus, 108, 142
Baëtis rhodani, 140, 144
Baëtis scambus, 108
Bainbridge, George, 15
Barker, Thomas, 9, 10, 13, 14
Barker's Delight, 10
Barlow, Bob, 36
Bi-visible hackles, 29
Black and Peacock Spider, 72, 73
Black Gnat, 12, 13, 48, 120, 121
Black Palmer, 110
Black Spider, 74
Black Wulff, 136
Black Zulu, 76, 77
Bloody Butcher, 80
Blue Charm, 48
Blue Dun, 12, 14, 16, 48, 56, 136
Blue Upright, 46, 62, 78, 79
Blue Winged Olive, 27, 48, 152, 160
Boke of St Albans, 7, 110
Bowlker, Charles, 13, 14, 15, 25
Bowlker, Richard, 13, 14, 15, 25
Bow-tie Buzzer, 24
Brachycentrus subnubilus, 130

British Museum, 21
Brown Fly, 14
Brown Wulff, 136
Burrard, Major Gerald, DSO, RFA (Retd), 23
Butcher (or Silver Butcher), 47, 80, 81

Cahill, Daniel, 29
Canham, Stuart, 27
Caperer (or Welshman's Button), 46, 122, 123
Capes (or Rooser Necks), 52-57
Centroptilum, 154
Certaine Experiments concerning Fish and Fruite: Practised by John Taverner, Gentleman, by him published for the benefit of others, 9
Chadwick's Wool, No. 477, 24
Chetham, James, 13, 98
Cholmondeley Pennell, 41
Claret Dun, 158
Clarke, Brian, 25-30, 54
Coachman, 46, 47, 82, 83
Coch-y-bondhu, 124, 125
Collyer, David, 138
Compleat Angler, 10, 11
Connemara Black, 84, 85
Cotton, Charles, 8, 11-14, 49, 110
Crane Fly (or Daddy-Long-Legs), 14, 126, 127
Cross, Reuben, 156

Daddy-Long-Legs (or Crane Fly), 14
Dame Juliana Berners, 7, 32
Dark Bloa, 48
Dark Cahill, 29, 148
Days and Nights of Salmon Fishing in the Tweed, 29
De natura animalium, 7
Dennis, Jack, 136
Diptera, 120
Dogsbody, 51
Donne Cutte, 8
Downs, Donald, 23
Drake Flye, 8
Draper, Keith, 31

Dry Fly Entomology, 128
Dry Fly Fishing in Theory and Practice, 19
Duffer's Fortnight, 112
Dun Cut, 8
Dun Drake, 14
Dung Fly, 8
Dunkeld, 86, 87
Dunne, J. W., 21
Dusky Yellowstreak, 104

Ecdyurus venosus, 98
Elements of Nymph Fishing, 25
English and Welsh Trout Flies, 25
Ephemera danica, 112
Ephemera lineata, 112
Ephemera vulgata, 112
Ephemerella ignita, 158
Ephemeroptera, 112, 148

Farlow, C. & Co., 21
February Red, 134
Fishing Gazette, 19, 20, 27
Floating Flies and how to dress them, 17
Fly-Dresser's Guide, 23
Fly-Dressing Materials, 24
Fly-Tying Development and Progress, 23
Fly-Tying for Trout, 22
Fly-Tying Materials, 56
Fly-tying: Principles and Practice, 23
Fly-Tying Problems, 23

Game and Gun, 23
Gapen, Don, 51
Gay, John, 6
Goddard, John, 25-30, 44, 142
Gold Ribbed Hare's Ear, 35, 50, 128, 129
Golden Olive, 88, 89
Gordon Quill (or Quill Gordon), 156
Gordon, Theodore, 29, 156
'Gossamer' Tying Silk, 42
Grannom, 8, 48, 130, 131
Great Red Spinner, 8
Green Drake, 12
Greentail Fly, 130
Greenwell, Canon William, 90, 132
Greenwell's Glory, 48, 90, 91
Greenwell, hackled variant, 132, 133
Grey Duster, 50, 55, 134, 135
Grey Goose, 24
Grey Palmer, 110
Grey Wulff, 49, 136, 137
Grouse and Green, 48, 92
Grouse Series, 92, 93

Hacklepoint Coachman, 110, 111
Halesus radiatus, 122
Halford, Michael Frederic, 17-19, 21-25, 122, 128, 134, 158
Hall, H. S., 17-19
Hardy Bros Ltd, 21
Harry-Long-Legs (or Daddy-Long-Legs), 14
Heckham Peckham, 47, 106
Hemming, David, 128
Herter, G. L., 128
Hewitt, Edward R., 29
Hilara maura, 120
Hills, Major J. W., 9
Hook scales, 41
Hooks, 37-42
How to Tie Flies for Trout and Grayling, 19

International Trout Flies, 25
Invicta, 47, 48, 94, 95
Iron Blue, 16, 27, 48, 104, 108, 142, 143
Ivens, Tom, 72, 86

Jamison, W. J., 40
Jenny Spinner, 16
Johnson, Frank, 30, 150
Jungle Alexandra, 70, 71

Kell, James, 27
Killer Bug, 24
Kite, Major Oliver, 24, 25
Kite's Imperial, 49, 140, 141

Lady of the Lake (see Alexandra), 70, 71
Large Dark Olive, 27, 48, 90, 140, 144, 145, 166
Large Red Spinner, 166
Last Hope, 146, 147
Lawrie, W. H., 25
Lead-wing Coachman, 82
Leiser, Eric, 56
Leptophlebia vespertina, 158
Lesser Hackle, 12
Light Blue Dun (or Pale Blue Dun), 55
Light Cahill, 29, 65, 148, 149
Little Blue Dun, 13
Little Claret, 142
Little Dorrit, 49, 65, 150, 151
Lunn, W. J., 48, 122
Lunn's Particular, 62

Mallard and Claret, 47, 58, 96, 97

'Marabou' Floss Silk, 42
March Brown, 8, 9, 47, 48, 98, 99
Marinaro, Vincent C., 26-28, 30
Marryat, George Selwyn, 17-19, 23
Marston, R. B., 27
Martin, Alexander, 28, 150
Mascall, Leonard, 9
Materials (plumage and fur), 46-52
Materials and Tools, 32-58
Mating Black Gnat, 120, 121
Matuka, 31
Mayfly, 8, 22, 39, 47, 112, 136
McClelland, Harry G., 19
Medium Olive, 90, 166
Minor Tactics of the Chalk Stream, 19, 20
Miscellaneous Aids, 36, 37
Modern Development of the Dry Fly, 18, 21
Modern Trout Flies, 25
Modern Trout Fly Dressing, 22
Mole Fly, 31
Monocord filament thread, 43
Mosely, Martin E., 21
Muddler Minnow, 51
Murdoch, William, 96

'Naples' Tying Silk, 42
North-Country Flies, 19
Nymph Fishing for Chalk Stream Trout, 20
Nymphs and the Trout, 24

Oak Fly, 8
Ogden, James, 94, 170
Olive Dun, 8
Olive Quill, 140
Olive (Red) Spinner, 22
Olive Upright, 104
Orange Quill, 50, 65, 152, 153
Orange Tag, 106

Pale Watery, 27, 146, 150, 154, 155
Palmer Fly (Flie), 10, 11, 76, 110
'Parachute' (style of hackle), 28, 36, 150, 164, 166
Partridge Hackle, 100
Partridge and Orange, 48, 100, 101
Partridge Spider, 100
Pearsall's tying silk, 42
Peter Ross, 48, 102, 103
Pheasant Tail, 104, 105
Phyllopertha horticola, 124
Picric acid, 49, 50, 57, 58
Plecoptera, 134

Poems, 6, 170
Pond Olive, 90
Pritt, T. E., 19, 25
Pulman, G. P. R., 16

Quill Gordon (or Gordon Quill), 29, 156, 157

Rat-Faced McDougal, 30
Red Hackle, 7
Red Palmer, 7, 110
Red Quill, 134, 158, 159
Red Spinner, 166
Red Tag, 7, 106, 107
Reservoir and Lake Flies, 23
Rhithrogena haarupi, 98
Richards, Carl, 30
Rogan, Michael, 34
Rogan's Olive (or Golden Olive), 47
Ronalds, Alfred, 16, 17, 25
Rooster Necks (or Capes), 52, 57
Rough Olive, 140
Royal Wulff, 136

Sandy Fly, 13
Sawyer, Frank, 24
Sawyer's Nymph, 47
Schwab, Peter, 30
Scotcher, George, 15
Scottish Trout Flies, 25
Scrope, William, 29
Sepia Dun, 104
Sericostoma personatum, 122
Sherry Spinner, 158, 160, 161
Silk, Fur and Feather, 20
Silver Butcher (or Butcher), 7, 47, 80, 81
Silver March Brown, 98
Simple Fredsedge, 47, 162, 163
Siphlonurus lacustris, 148
Siphlonurus quebecensis, 148
Skues, George Edward Mackenzie, 19-21, 23, 26, 78, 98, 152
Small Brown, 134
Small Dark Olive, 108, 166
Small Red Spinner, 166
Small Spurwing, 104
Snipe and Orange, 108
Snipe and Purple, 108, 109
Snipe and Yellow, 108
Soldier Palmer, 7, 66, 110, 111
Stenonema ithaca, 148
Stewart, W. C., 74
Stillwater Fly-Fishing, 72
Stoddart, James Tod, 15

Stonefly, 8, 12, 100, 134
Straddlebug Mayfly (or Summer Duck), 47, 112, 113
Sunshine and the Dry Fly, 21
Swisher, Doug, 30

Taupo Tiger, 31
Taverner, Eric, 22, 26
Taverner, John, 9
Teal and Black, 114
Teal and Red, 102
Teal, Blue and Silver, 114, 115
Teal Series, 48, 114, 115
The Angler's Vade Mecum, 13
The Art of Angling (Barker, T.), 9
The Art of Angling (Bowlker, R. & C.), 13
The Art of Angling as Practised in Scotland, 15
The Dry-Fly Fisherman's Entomology, 21
The Dry-fly Man's Handbook, 19
The Fly-Dresser's Birds, 20
The Fly Fisher's Entomology, 16
The Fly-Fisher's Guide, 15
The Fly-Fisher's Legacy, 15
The Manner of Making the Artificial Fly, 14
The Natural Trout Fly and its Imitation, 21
The Pursuit of Still-water Trout, 25
The Practical Angler, 74
The Trout and the Fly, 26
The Vade-Mecum of Fly-Fishing for Trout, 16, 17
The Way of a Trout with a Fly, 20, 26
Theakston, Michael, 17
Thompson vice, 34
Threads, Tinsels, Wires, Wax and Varnish, 42-45
Tiahape Tickler, 31
Tools, 33-35
Tools and Materials, 32-58
Treacle Parkin, 106
'Treatyse of Fysshynge with an Angle,' 8-10, 14, 15, 25

Trichoptera, 130
Trout 'cone of vision' and 'window,' 26, 27
Trout Fishing from all Angles, 22, 26
Trout Flies of New Zealand, 31
Trout Flies of Still Water, 25
Trout Fly Recognition, 25, 142

USD Paradun, 30, 54
USD Para-olive, 27, 28, 164, 165
USD Poly-red Spinner, 36, 65, 166, 167

Van Conson (Skues, G.E.M.), 20
Veniard, John, 23, 34, 35

Walker, Richard, 25, 66, 168
Walker's Sedge, 168, 169
Walton, Izaak, 10, 11, 32, 98, 110
Waspe Fly (or Waspe Flye), 8, 14
Waterhen Bloa, 48
Waterwalkers, 30, 150
Ways and means, 59-68
Welshman's Button (or Caperer), 122, 123
West, Leonard, 21
Western Trout Fly Tying Manual, 136
Wheatly, Hewett, 17
Whip finish (sequences of), 67
Whisky Fly, 49
White Wulff, 136
Wickham's Fancy, 48, 116, 117
Williams, A. Courtney, 104, 106, 108
Willow Fly, 134
Woodcock and Green, 48, 118, 119
Woodcock and Red, 118
Woodcock Series, 48
Woodcock and Yellow, 118
Woolley, Roger, 22, 25
Worcester Gem, 106
Wulff, Lee, 30, 49, 136
Wynkyn de Worde, 8

Yellow May Dun, 8
Yorkshire Trout Flies, 19